Data Center

From Beginner to Professional

3-book boxset comprising of:

Data Center for Beginners
Designing Datacenters – Book 1: Power
Designing Datacenters – Book 2: Cooling

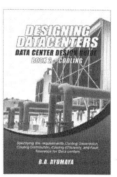

B.A. AYOMAYA

DISCLAIMER

All material used is original work or it has come from public domain sources e.g. the Internet. Should any copyright owner wish to have any items removed, then please contact the author at the following address: dcbadru@gmail.com.

Every effort has been made to provide accurate and complete information. However, the author assumes no responsibility for any direct, indirect, incidental, or consequential damages arising from the use of the information in this document.

Copyright © 2021 Badrudeen Ajibola Ayomaya.
All rights reserved.

No part of this publication may be reproduced, transmitted, transcribed, stored in a retrieval system, or translated into any language or computer language, in any form or by any means; electronic, mechanical, magnetic, chemical, thermal, manual, or otherwise, without the prior consent in writing of the copyright owner. Applications for the copyright owner's permission to reproduce any part of this publication should be sent to the copyright owner by email at the following address: dcbadru@gmail.com.

The book is sold subject to the condition that it shall not by way of trade, or otherwise, be lent, re-sold, hired out, or otherwise circulated without the copyright owner's prior consent in writing in any form of binding or cover other than in which it is published and without a similar condition including this condition being imposed on the subsequent purchaser.

Printed and published in the United States of America.

ISBN: 9798736694389

CONTENTS

Data Center for Beginners

DESIGNING DATA CENTERS; Data Center Design Guide – Book 1: Power

DESIGNING DATA CENTERS; Data Center Design Guide – Book 2: Cooling

B.A. Ayomaya

A beginner's guide
towards understanding
Data Center Design

Data Center for Beginners

Data Center for Beginners

A beginner's guide towards understanding data center design

B.A. AYOMAYA

DISCLAIMER

All material used is original work or it has come from public domain sources e.g. the Internet. Should any copyright owner wish to have any items removed, then please contact the author at the following address: dcbadru@gmail.com.

Every effort has been made to provide accurate and complete information. However, the author assumes no responsibility for any direct, indirect, incidental, or consequential damages arising from the use of the information in this document.

Copyright © 2017 Badrudeen Ajibola Ayomaya.
All rights reserved.

No part of this publication may be reproduced, transmitted, transcribed, stored in a retrieval system, or translated into any language or computer language, in any form or by any means; electronic, mechanical, magnetic, chemical, thermal, manual, or otherwise, without the prior consent in writing of the copyright owner. Applications for the copyright owner's permission to reproduce any part of this publication should be sent to the copyright owner by email at the following address: **dcbadru@gmail.com**.

The book is sold subject to the condition that it shall not by way of trade, or otherwise, be lent, re-sold, hired out, or otherwise circulated without the copyright owner's prior consent in writing in any form of binding or cover other than in which it is published and without a similar condition including this condition being imposed on the subsequent purchaser.

Printed and published in the United States of America.

ISBN 9781520527079

"It is not the critic who counts; not the man who points out how the strong man stumbles, or where the doer of deeds could have done them better. The credit belongs to the man who is actually in the arena, whose face is marred by dust and sweat and blood; who strives valiantly; who errs, who comes short again and again, because there is no effort without error and shortcoming; but who does actually strive to do the deeds; who knows great enthusiasms, the great devotions; who spends himself in a worthy cause; who at the best knows in the end the triumph of high achievement, and who at the worst, if he fails, at least fails while daring greatly, so that his place shall never be with those cold and timid souls who neither know victory nor defeat."

- Theodore Roosevelt

CONTENTS

Welcome to This Guide viii
INTRODUCTION 1
  DEFINITION 1
    To Build or Not To Build 5
      Managed Hosting Platforms 5
      Co-location Data Centers 6
      Enterprise Data Centers 6
    Site Selection 7
  COMPONENTS IN THE DATA CENTER 10
    Data Center Spaces 12
    IT Equipment 14
    Facility Equipment 15
    POWER 16
    Power Path Elements 18
      Utility Supply 18
      Generators 18
      Transfer Switches 18
      Distribution Panel 19
      UPS 19
      PDU 20

- More About UPS 22
  - Offline UPS 23
  - Line Interactive 24
  - Online Double conversion UPS 25
  - Online Delta conversion UPS 26
- Rotary UPS Systems 27
- COOLING 30
  - Room Cooling 31
  - Row Cooling 31
  - Rack Cooling 31
- Heat Removal Techniques 32
- Humidity 34
- Considerations for Energy Efficiency 36
  - Virtualization 37
  - Ventilation 37
  - Aisle Arrangement 38
  - Sealed Rooms 39
  - Airflow Management 39
  - Cable Management 39
  - Aisle Containment 39
  - CRAC vs CRAH 41
- ANCILLARY SYSTEMS 42
- DATA CENTER STANDARDS 43

    Standard Bodies 43
    Uptime Institute 44
    TIA 45
    BICSI 46
    ASHRAE 47
NEXT STEPS 49
BIBLIOGRAPHY 51

Welcome to This Guide

If you are reading these words, it means you are interested in Data Centers. You may be an experienced Data Center professional, a novice just wondering what Data Centers are all about, or perhaps you've read a few things about Data Centers, and are wondering whether to pursue a career in this field. Either way, this guide will help provide some information.

I have been in the Data Center industry for about a decade. I have often seen people succumb to the hype and delve into often expensive training and certifications, only to find out that they are not cut out for this path.

The Data Center industry is a highly technical, highly practical, niche-based industry requiring costly investments across all verticals – including training, designing, building, and maintenance. As such, it is always beneficial to have a general overview of what the Data Center is all about, before committing to the path.

This short guide attempts to give that general overview, providing a few tidbits and advice along the way.

I hope it proves to be a valuable companion as you take your career to the next level.

Sincerely yours
B. A. Ayomaya

INTRODUCTION

The traditional data center is undergoing many changes, if not a revolution. Hybrid cloud infrastructures, hosted servers, virtualized servers and new methods to save energy and reduce costs in the data center create an ever-challenging array of decisions for today's data center managers.

DEFINITION

Several definitions exist for the Data Center. TIA 942 defines a Data Center as "a building or portion of a building whose primary purpose is to house a computer room and its support areas".

The Data Center is also defined as a facility used to house computer systems and associated components, such as telecommunications and storage systems. It generally includes redundant backup power supplies, redundant communications connections, environmental controls (e.g. air conditioning, fire suppression), and various security devices.

Others define it as a centralized repository, either physical or virtual, for the storage, management, and dissemination of data and information organized around a particular body of knowledge or pertaining to a particular Business.

So, what is a Data Center? I will leave the particular wordings to you as long as you understand the concepts. Now let me tell you a story.

Imagine you came across an interesting idea that helps you make money. You set up a service you offer people. You enthusiastically run around offering this service. Eventually, you got tired of running around rendering this service manually and sat down thinking of what to do.

Your friend introduced you to this amazing machine. This machine can do anything and everything you ask it to do, at breathtaking speed. You marvel at this discovery and ponder about how to pass your message across to the machine. You set out to the land of magicians, a.k.a. IT guys. Eventually, you get some magicians (programmers) to tell the computer all about your Business and how it works. Now the machine can render the service while you go riding your bicycle.

However, you can't just leave this life-saving machine on your desk! You take it to a cozy hut where it can rule in all its glory. You set up cooling for it, so it can keep crunching away without bothering about the heat. Then you think: my clients need to reach the machine. Even when they reach the machine, I need to store all the information processed somewhere. You return to the land

INTRODUCTION

of magicians. The head magician tells you to calm down. He then proceeds to send some of the magicians along with you. These other magicians (network and storage administrators) bring strange-looking equipment to the hut, do some mumbo jumbo involving tying some sort of ropes, and tell you outsiders can now connect to your machine. Also, your information can now be stored.

You try to power on the machine, but it does not respond. You ask the magicians to help you, but they say it is none of their Business. They direct you to some guys called Facility Managers.

These people come and bring some groggy looking equipment to the hut. They place these equipment in other rooms and do another ropey mumbo jumbo – except that these ropes are heavier and bulkier than the IT Guys'. Eventually, they complete their job. The computer powers on, your clients can reach it remotely and it happily renders the services. You are so elated, and you go ride your bicycle.

Moral of the Story:

The machine that does your services for you is called a **Server**

The equipment that let your client communicate with your Server are called **Switches**

The equipment that stores your information are collectively called **Storage**.

These three groups of equipment are collectively called: **IT Equipment**

All the other equipment that support the operation of the IT Equipment are collectively called **Facility Equipment**

The ropes used by the IT Guys are called **Data Cables**

The bulkier ropes used by the Facility Guys are called **Power Cables**

The room where you keep the Server, Switches, and Storage is called the **Computer Room**

The rooms where you keep the Facility Equipment are called the **Support Areas**

That fancy hut of yours is known as the **DATA CENTER**.

The Data Center is that building that houses the Computer Room and its Support Areas[1], so that your services can run continuously and efficiently.

---

[1] This is the TIA 942 definition

INTRODUCTION

To Build or Not To Build

We have seen that the Data Center exists because of the Business. But the Business itself exists only to make money. It makes no sense therefore for the Data Center to gulp all the money the Business makes, which would be the case if we all had to build our own individual Data Centers.

Luckily, humans are really smart animals. Some people already had this problem way before you started reading this guide. Solving this resulted in the three categories of Data Centers. These are:

- Managed Hosting Platform
- Colocation Data Centers
- Enterprise Data Centers

Managed Hosting Platforms or Services or Facilities are Data Centers managed by a Third Party on behalf of a Business. The Business does not own or control the Data Center or any space within the Data Center. Rather, the Business rents IT equipment and infrastructure it needs instead of investing in outright purchases at one go.

The Business has an agreement with the Third Party owning the facility that guarantees the uptime of the IT infrastructure rented. The health of the equipment, power, cooling, and other support infrastructure are wholly managed by the Third Party.

This approach could lead to real cost savings especially when the required equipment has a small footprint. It could also be a real advantage when the Business wants to completely concentrate on its core offerings, rather than worry about managing facilities.

Co-location Data Centers are (usually large) facilities built to accommodate multiple Businesses. The Business rents its own space within Data Center, and subsequently fills the space with its IT equipment. However, it is not unusual for the Co-location operator to provide some of the IT equipment required.

As with Managed Hosting, the Business has a standing agreement with the Co-location provider guaranteeing the operation of the other support facilities (Power, Cooling, etc.), which are provided and managed by the Co-location operator.

This approach allows for greater control by the Business of its Digital Assets. The Business also chooses its operational environment and infrastructure options.

Enterprise Data Centers are facilities wholly built, maintained, operated and managed by the Business for the optimal operation of its IT equipment. It is usually a highly capital intensive asset that guarantees the complete control of the operational and security of Digital Assets. The Business also controls the reliability, availability, and integration of its facility.

INTRODUCTION

This approach can be a liability if the Business does not possess the necessary expertise to run the Data Center through the Design, Construction, Operation and Maintenance phases. The design of Enterprise Data Centers is the focus of this guide.

Site Selection

Ofcourse, a critical factor that determines if a data center will achieve the objectives for which it is built is its location. A data center built to support systems that analyze and predict security threats should not be easily at the reach of security threats.

The decision on which location to site the data center is critical as it directly affects the total cost of building and operating the data center, as well as its effective lifespan. There are many factors to consider when making this decision.

The most obvious is the availability and cost of real estate. The closer it gets to urban centers and coastal areas, the more expensive land becomes. Data centers with very high capacity needs might have no choice but to be set up in rural areas.

Another important factor is connectivity. Services produced in the data center can only get to the users through a network. Availability of fiber networks and other telecommunications point of presence with acceptable cost and latency limits and must be ascertained in advance.

Power accounts for the majority of the data center operating costs. Availability of utility power with tolerable costs and tariffs is an important selection factor.

With the global focus on energy efficiency and green initiatives, an important factor for site selection is the type of environment. A site that allows for the use of clean, renewable energy sources and other energy-efficiency tactics like air-water economization is becoming more attractive to data center owners.

The environment's susceptibility to natural disasters must also be investigated. Likewise, the site needs to be safe from man-made disasters like accidents, plane crashes, and terrorist activities.

The wellbeing of the data center operations staff is also paramount. The site should be easily accessible with allowable commute times to and from residential areas. Crime rates and costs of living should be considered as well.

Laws, regulations, and taxes from Authorities Having Jurisdiction (AHJs) must be diligently studied prior to site selection. There may also be economic incentives from governments seeking to boost employment rates.

INTRODUCTION

It can be seen from the above that data center site selection is not an activity that can be taken lightly[2]. All stakeholders must painstakingly consider the factors and arrive at a solution that meets data center strategic objectives.

---

[2] The ANSI/TIA 942 Standard provides an informative annex for data center site selection and other building design considerations. This source can be consulted for further insights.

COMPONENTS IN THE DATA CENTER

So we have taken a brief overview of what the Data Center is all about. It's time to go into a little bit more detail.

It is important to note that the Data Center does not exist for and of itself. Its role is to support the technology that supports the Business.

Because all modern Businesses are driven by some form of technology, it is pertinent that this technology suffers little to no downtime. The technology needs to be housed in an infrastructure that keeps it running as long as the Business runs. The role of the Data Center is therefore very critical to the operational and survival of the Business.

Every Data Center is not the same. Not every Data Center needs to have the same attributes. As the Data Center exists because of the Business, its remains logical that the components of the Data Center be defined by the needs of the Business.

So what are the things the Business needs the Data Center for? The Data Center is a place to:

- Locate the Servers, Switches, and Storage equipment
- Provide appropriate environmental conditions for the optimal running of the IT equipment (Servers, Storage and Switches)

- Provide a way for internal and external customers to reach the Servers
- Provide power in appropriate capacity and duration for the IT equipment to continuously run

So you see, the Data Center is not an office. Typically, the Data Center should be completely devoid of human presence.

Components in the Data Center include:

- IT Equipment
- Facility Equipment
- Ancillary Systems

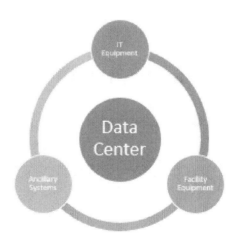

Figure 1: Data Center Components

Data Center Spaces

Obviously, these three different categories of equipment cannot be left jumbled up and standing right next to each other. There needs to be a structure around the location and positioning of these equipment.

The Telecommunications Industry Association (TIA) in its data center standard, the TIA-942-A[3], proposes the structure below:

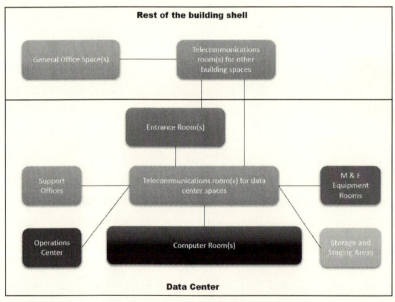

Data Center Spaces

---

[3] The TIA and its data center standard are discussed in later sections of this book.

COMPONENTS IN THE DATA CENTER 13

According to the standard, the part of the building referred to as the data center should have dedicated spaces for:

Operations monitoring, where an eye is kept on every minute detail and important metrics of the data center operations;

Support offices, where support and maintenance staff can sit;

M & E equipment rooms, where mechanical and electrical equipment are kept;

Storage and Staging Areas, where equipment are stored and loaded into the data center;

Computer rooms, where the actual critical IT equipment are kept;

Entrance rooms, where external service provider equipment are kept; and

Telecommunications rooms, where network access to resources in these different spaces are managed.

Other areas in the building are served through dedicated telecommunications rooms that access data center services through the data center telecommunication rooms.

The design, sizing, and location of these different spaces are important aspects to be sorted out during the early stages of the data center design phase. Constraints should be identified and overcome jointly by qualified external professionals e.g. architects and structural engineers, and internal stakeholders e.g. IT department, Facilities department, Security department, etc.

The starting point would evidently be the required data center capacity. This would determine the space needed, the total number of IT equipment, and the total number of Facility equipment required. This will also drive the business decision to either build out an enterprise data center or rent from a colocation provider.

IT Equipment

From the previous scenario, we see that traditionally, IT Equipment consists primary of Servers, Switches and Storage equipment. However, with recent pull towards technologies like the Virtualization and the Cloud, coupled with the need to reduce equipment footprint and power consumption, these lines are starting to blur.

There is distinct trend showing the adoption of Converged, Hyper-converged and Web-scale infrastructure. We are heading to an era where Servers, Switches and Storage are treated as roles spread across

COMPONENTS IN THE DATA CENTER 15

different hardware rather than distinct elements tied to specific hardware[4].

However, there are still many datacenters operating traditionally. The hardware manufacturers will not stop churning out dedicated Server, Storage and Switching equipment anytime soon.

The discussion of the different types, capacities, specifications and considerations for IT equipment is beyond the scope of this document. These will be treated in detail in a subsequent publication.

Facility Equipment

Recall that we defined Facility Equipment as "all other equipment that support the operation of the IT equipment". Now, the critical support IT equipment require to function are twofold: Power and Cooling. It follows therefore that Facility Equipment are those that provide Power and Cooling to the critical spaces occupied by the IT Equipment, within the Data Center.

Facility Equipment provide Power and Cooling to the critical spaces within the Data Center.

---

[4] These are hardware types that combine roles of a Server with Storage and/or Switching and Management

POWER

All IT Equipment in the Data Center require electrical power to function. Likewise, all other facility equipment not providing power, e.g. cooling and lighting, require power as well. Therefore, the designer, when planning for Data Center power during the design phase, should account for power consumption by both sets of equipment. Typically, the total power supplied to the Data Center should be two times or more the total power required by the IT equipment (including future Loads). The other half will be consumed by the cooling and other facilities.

The subject of Power is a highly technical and professional one governed by local legal codes, regional and international standards, as well as industry best practices. We will not concern ourselves with discussions of detailed complexities that are more suited to a dedicated course. Rather, our focus is a general understanding of Power requirements in the Data Center.

Now that we realize that our IT equipment requires Power, how do we quantify the Power required?

Power is usually measured in Watts (W). Each IT equipment has a specific Wattage, or Power Rating, specifying the amount of Power it consumes. The total sum of Power Ratings of all IT equipment running in the Data Center gives the total IT Load of the Data Center.

COMPONENTS IN THE DATA CENTER

IT Load, or Critical Load, is the total Power consumed by all critical IT equipment in the Data Center.

It is quite difficult to accurately predict the actual IT equipment that will be operation during the lifespan of the Data Center. As such, another metric for determining the power requirements of the Data Center from inception is required. As most IT equipment are typically mounted in racks and cabinets, power requirements are typically measured in Watts (W) or Kilowatts (kW) per rack. This is the collective sum of the power requirements of all IT equipment mounted on that rack[5].

Industry best practice is to allocate 4 -5 kW per rack. The number of racks deployed in the Data Center can then be limited by the amount of power available[6]. The reverse can also apply i.e. the amount of racks the Data Center space can accommodate determines the amount of Power to be provided to the Data Center[7].

---

[5] Most manufacturer specified power requirements for IT equipment are usually over-stated. Actual consumption typically does not exceed 70% of stated value. A good practice is to de-rate stated values by 60 – 70% before computing total IT Load

[6] For example, if 25kW of Power is available, 12.5kW will be used by IT Equipment. This means a maximum of 3 racks in the Data Center

[7] For example, if after considering free movement and air flow, a computer room can accommodate 10 racks conveniently, the power provided to the room should be in excess of 100kW

Power Path Elements

The path through which Power flows to the Data Center consists of the following elements and more:

- Utility Supply
- Generators
- Transfer Switches
- Distribution Panels
- Uninterruptible Power Supply (UPS)
- PDU

Utility Supply is the power supply to the Data Center sourced from the public distribution grid. It is controlled by the government or public power distribution companies and is not considered a reliable source for powering the Data Center. They are however utilized to minimize the costs of providing power to the Data Center.

Generators are machines used to generate electrical Power. They convert mechanical energy, usually from motors, to the electrical energy used to power the Data Center. They are the primary source of Power to the Data Center, since they are completely in the control of the Data Center Operators.

Transfer Switches are electrical switches used to transfer electric Load from one power source to the other. The transfer could be from one utility line to another, from engine-generators to utility and vice versa, or between two generators. The transfer could be manually activated. It could also be automatic when Automatic Transfer Switches (ATS) or Static Transfer Switches (STS) are used.

Distribution Panel as the name implies is an enclosure wherein a single electrical power feed is divided into separate subsidiary circuits for feeding multiple distinct Loads. The circuits may all be of equal or differing capacities. Each circuit or power feed is protected by a circuit breaker or an electrical fuse to prevent the end electrical Loads from over-drawing power beyond specified limits

UPS means Uninterruptible Power Supply. The UPS is an electrical device that provides continuous power to a Load even when the mains power source is unavailable. It works by storing electrical energy in backup devices, such as batteries, from input power. The UPS then supplies the Load with the stored energy almost instantaneously when the input power is cut off.

The expected runtime of a UPS supply power from backed-up source is not expected to last long, as this is supposed to be an emergency measure while the mains power source, from Utility or Generator, can be restored.

Another important function of the UPS is to clean out and stabilize the power from the mains supply. The power from the mains supply can be subject to fluctuations in form, voltage, and frequency owing to interference or generation conditions. The UPS has the ability to correct some of these anomalies.

The UPS is especially important for the protection of IT and other equipment that are highly sensitive to Power disruption and irregularities.

PDU means Power Distribution Unit. The PDU distributes power to the individual pieces of equipment. The PDUs come in various sizes and forms, with some being rack-mountable while others occupy Data Center whitespace.

The figure below shows a simple flow of Power to the Critical IT Load in the Data Center. In reality, some Data Center deployments are a lot more complex. However, all designs are built from the same foundation components.

COMPONENTS IN THE DATA CENTER

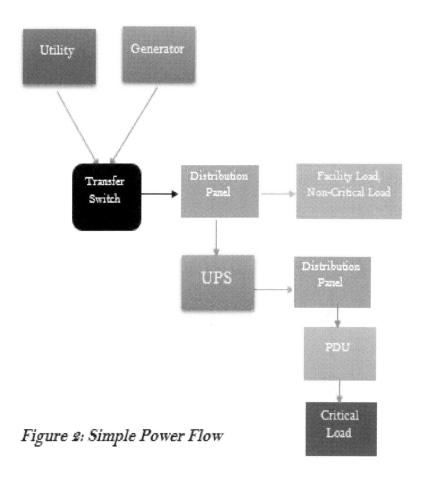

Figure 2: Simple Power Flow

More About UPS

As UPS is a crucial component in the Data Center, they deserve slightly more than a passing treatment. We will now take a closer look at UPS Systems.

There are two types of UPS Systems: Static UPS and Rotary UPS

Static UPS Systems are so named because they have no moving parts throughout the power flow. They typically store electricity in the form of chemical energy in batteries. This UPS system has three main components:

- The rectifier, which converts AC from the mains into DC
- The storage medium, which stores the converted DC. The most common form for storing electrical energy is through batteries[8]
- The inverter, which converts stored DC to AC for supply to the electrical load

There are varying configurations that determine the way Power is routed to the Load. This leads to further sub-categorization as follows:

---

[8] The type of batteries used are telecom grade, rechargeable, Valve Regulated Lead Acid (VRLA) batteries

COMPONENTS IN THE DATA CENTER

Offline UPS

Here, the Load is powered directly from the mains when the mains input is present. The UPS switches the Load over to the battery when the mains input goes off.

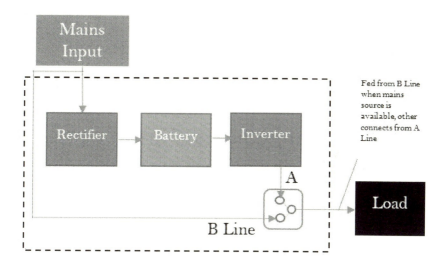

Figure 3: Offline UPS

There is a noticeable time lag during the switching process. More so, the irregularities (if any) in the mains power are carried over to the Load. These make this configuration not conducive for sensitive critical Load.

Line Interactive

This configuration is similar to the Offline system. However, a voltage regulator is introduced after the mains just before the Load.

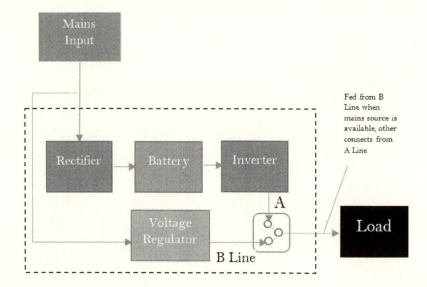

Figure 4: Line Interactive UPS

The Voltage Regulator corrects some of the irregularities, but cannot correct frequency. There is still a noticeable time lag during the switching process. Critical Load is not to be powered with this system.

COMPONENTS IN THE DATA CENTER

Online Double conversion UPS

This configuration completely isolates the Load from the mains input. The Load is always fed from the DC Power.

The AC power from the mains is converted to DC to keep the batteries charged. The inverter then converts the DC back to AC to supply the Load.

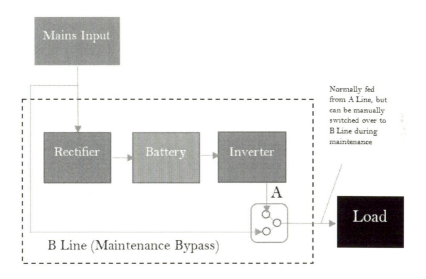

Figure 5: Online Double Conversion UPS

This ensures that the supply to the Load is always clean and continuous, making it suitable to critical Data Center Loads. A bypass is included so that the Load can be switched manually switched over to the mains supply temporarily during maintenance operations.

One drawback however is that this configuration is not very efficient due to losses accrued during the conversion processes.

Online Delta conversion UPS

This is a variation of Line Interactive system. It uses a Delta Converter in place of the Voltage Regulator.

The Delta Conversion UPS allows a portion of the Load to be fed from the mains, while the rest is fed from the Inverter. This allows the stabilization of the output voltage. It also ensures that there is no switching time lag if the mains input is cut, as the Inverter can seamlessly assume the rest of the Load.

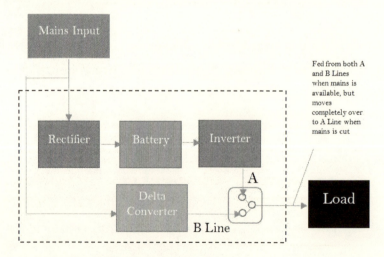

Figure 6: Online Delta Conversion UPS

COMPONENTS IN THE DATA CENTER

This configuration provides the greatest efficiency. However, frequency anomalies cannot be corrected[9].

Rotary UPS Systems

Rotary UPS Systems are so named because they store electrical energy in the form of kinetic energy.

The incoming mains supply drives a motor which in turn spins an electro-mechanical flywheel at a very high rate. The flywheel drives an electrical generator to provide power to the Load, while at the same time storing Kinetic Energy. Once power failure occurs, the Kinetic Energy in the flywheel is released to drive the generator, so that it continues to power the Load, providing a ride-through period within which the backup generator can be started.

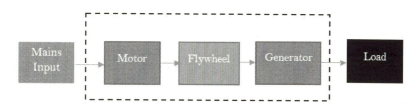

Figure 7: Rotary UPS

Some variations add batteries to the flywheel for energy storage. Another variation incorporates a Diesel Generator into the Rotary UPS System. Once the power

---

[9] In some installations, a Mains Correction Panel is introduced before the UPS to correct frequency irregularities

outage exceeds a few seconds, the Diesel Generator is started to provide the input power. This precludes the need for an external backup generator. This system is known as Diesel Rotary UPS (DRUPS) system.

There has been an ongoing argument[10] about which UPS system is best suited for Data Center functions. While Static UPS systems dominate the existing Data Center deployments, there is still much benefit Rotary UPS system can offer. Manufacturers of both systems continue to advance arguments supporting their chosen lines.

Rotary UPS systems are usually manufactured for higher power ranges (200kW and above). DRUPS systems are generally not found in capacities lower than 500kW.

Rotary systems provide little ride-through time (about 15 seconds) compared to Static systems, which can backup power for up to 30 minutes. Also, Rotary systems require vigorous maintenance regimes, unlike Static systems, which most times just need routine cleaning.

On the other hand, Rotary systems allow for massive savings in expensive Data Center space. They also have a considerable lifespan compared to Static UPS system components.

---

[10] An interesting discussion can be seen in the APC white paper #92 "A Comparison of Static and Rotary UPS", freely downloadable from www.apc.com

In all cases, the choice of UPS system to utilize will depend on what system suits the Business objective better.

COOLING

Cooling in the Data Center is very important, perhaps even more important than Power itself. This is because in the absence of cooling, even in the presence of power, data center temperatures can rise at a rate of 30% after every minute. This will not only shut down IT equipment as they reach inoperable environmental considerations but could also lead to damage with burnt internal components. It is a high priority for every Data Center Manager to ensure there is adequate cooling while the IT equipment are powered up.

With a component as critical as this, it is natural for bodies are formed to recommend best practices for Data Centers. The most recognizable of these bodies is ASHRAE[11].

The heat generated for IT equipment operation, coupled with basic room temperature, is responsible for the high-temperature levels in the Data Center. Cooling in the Data Center is simply the removal of heat from the Data Center to the outside environment. This removal is handled by equipment called Computer Room Air Conditioners (CRACs) or Computer Room Air Handlers (CRAHs), depending on the method of removal. ASHRAE recommends that the Data Center critical areas be kept at a temperature range of 18°C and 27°C.

---

[11] American Society of Heating, Refrigerating, and Air-Conditioning Engineers (ASHRAE)

There are three primary ways this cooling can be achieved: Room Cooling, Row Cooling, and Rack Cooling.

Room Cooling

In this approach, cooling is provided for the room as a whole. This method can be suitable for small data centers, but decidedly become more cumbersome as the data center density increases. This is because the air conditioners have to constantly stir and mix the air in the room to prevent hot-spots and bring it to a common regular temperature.

Row Cooling

In this approach, cooling is provided on a row by row basis. This allows each row to run different load densities, so that differing cooling intensities can be applied as required.

Hot-spot and cooling irregularities can be easily managed by proper layout and equipment placement.

Rack Cooling

In this approach, cooling is provided on a rack by rack basis. Specific air-conditioning units are dedicated to specific racks. This approach allows for maximum densities to be deployed per rack. However, this advantage can only be realized in data centers with fully loaded racks, otherwise, there would be too much cooling capacity, and air-conditioning losses alone can exceed total IT load.

There is no best method – the cooling approach should depend on the peculiarities of the data center. It is desirable to combine different approaches in one data center for the highest cooling efficiency. However, we find that design trends favor the row-based approach. This is probably the safest option.

Heat Removal Techniques

From Physics, we learn that heat can only flow in one direction – from hot to cold. We also learn heat can be transferred either by Conduction, Convection, or Radiation.

Conduction is the transfer of heat through a solid material, known as a conductor. Convection is the transfer of heat through the movement of a liquid or gas. Radiation is the transfer of heat by means of electromagnetic waves, emitted due to the temperature difference between two objects.

Convection is the method used to transfer heat away from the data center. This transfer is done through a process known as the Refrigeration Cycle.

The Refrigeration Cycle is a cycle of Evaporation, Compression, Condensation, and Expansion of a fluid or gas. This fluid or gas is known as the Refrigerant. The Refrigeration Cycle effectively transfers heat away from the data center into the external environment.

Through the different stages of the refrigeration cycle, the refrigerant's physical state oscillates between liquid and gas.

Evaporation will absorb heat from the data center environment and turn the refrigerant into a gas. This heat in the gaseous refrigerant is channeled to the compressor

Compression will apply pressure to the gaseous refrigerant, making it absorb much more heat thereby causing its internal temperature to rise. This hot gaseous refrigerant is channeled to the condenser in the next phase of eliminating data center heat.

Condensation will pass heat from the high-temperature high-pressure gas to the outside air. As heat flows from the hot region to the cold region, outside air is directed to the condensation coil. The refrigerant flowing through the coil then transfers heat to the outside air, which is then channeled out to the outdoor environment. The refrigerant then becomes a hot, high-pressure liquid.

Expansion will reduce the pressure in the refrigerant thereby reducing the temperature. This ends the cycle with the refrigerant returning to a cold liquid. The cycle is then restarted.

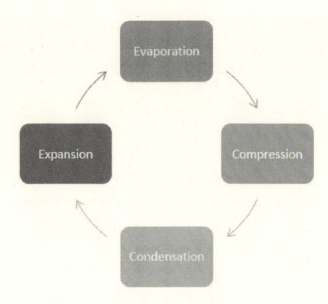

Figure 8: Refrigeration Cycle

Another method of removing heat from the data center is via Chilled Water Systems. This method, while more efficient and cost-effective than direct expansion systems using the refrigeration cycle, is much more complex. It utilizes fans and cooling coils to remove heat from the data center via chilled water.

Humidity

Like temperature, humidity[12] is also an important environmental factor in the data center. Regulating

---

[12] Amount of water vapour in air

COMPONENTS IN THE DATA CENTER

humidity is critical. Too low humidity levels affect the incidence of static electricity, which is an electric charge at rest. This electric charge can lead to an Electrostatic Discharge (ESD), which could cause significant damage to IT equipment. Too high humidity can cause water condensation on IT equipment, which could lead to water dropping on the chips in equipment, resulting in the current short-circuit.

In measuring humidity, the terms Relative Humidity, Dew Point, and Saturation are used.

Relative humidity is the amount of water vapor in the air as a percentage of the maximum amount of water vapor the air can hold at a given temperature. It follows that relative humidity can vary as the air temperature changes. e.g. at a higher temperature, air will expand causing it to be able to hold more water, thus relative humidity becomes lower. The reverse is the case at higher temperatures. ASHRAE recommends maximum relative humidity levels of 60%.

Dew point is the exact temperature where relative humidity becomes 100%. At this point, the water vapor leaves the air and appears as liquid water droplets on any object in the data center. ASHRAE recommends a maximum of 15.50C dew point. The air is said to be "saturated" at this temperature.

Humidity in the data center is regulated using Precision Cooling units, which regulate temperature and water vapor levels in the environment.

Humidification/Dehumidification systems are used. These produce/reduce water vapor in the atmosphere to the desired quantities.

In addition to humidity regulation equipment, the following practices should be followed to restrict fluctuation in humidity levels:

- Reduce the frequency of entry/exit into/from the data center. Constant opening of data center entrances can lead to infiltration of warmer air from outside, which could destabilize the environment
- Seal perimeter infiltrations and entrance points that lead to uncontrolled environments
- Seal doorways to guard against air and vapor leaks
- Paint perimeter walls to the penetration of moisture
- Avoid unnecessary openings

Considerations for Energy Efficiency

The above has been a discussion of Power and Cooling, which together make up the total energy consumption in the data center. With rising energy costs, it becomes necessary to find and implement approaches for reducing energy consumption in the data center. The following will review common strategies for achieving this aim.

Virtualization

Perhaps one of the most important concepts of the last century, Virtualization has revolutionized the way IT operates and provisions servers.

Virtualization allows the creation of several virtual entities sharing the same physical resources while appearing on the network as separate physical entities.

Traditionally, each service to be provided by the data center is tied to specific server hardware. Often, this hardware can provide much more processing power than the service requires, leading to redundant server abilities. The server hardware consumes almost the same power regardless of the utilization efficiency.

With the advent of virtualization, however, more than one service can be run on a single hardware, thus providing the multiple benefits of an increase in hardware efficiency, a significant reduction in total power consumption, and lower space usage in the data center.

Ventilation

As IT equipment take in cooling from the front and discharge from the back, the cabinets where they are housed must be properly ventilated.

The front, and back, of the cabinet need to be adequately perforated to allow a good flow of air through to the equipment.

Aisle Arrangement

As discussed in an earlier section, it is advantageous to provide cooling on a row-by-row basis. Taking this further, many standard bodies, including TIA and ASHRAE, recommend arranging racks and cabinets in the hot-aisle cold-aisle alignment.

In this arrangement, the racks are in each row are arranged such that the front and backs of adjacent rows face each other. This leads to a repeatable sequence after every 7 tiles, known as the 7 pitch tile rule.

If cold air is channeled to the front of the racks with this arrangement, the aisle between rack fronts facing each other is distinctly cold (cold aisle), while that at rack backs is distinctly hot (hot aisle).

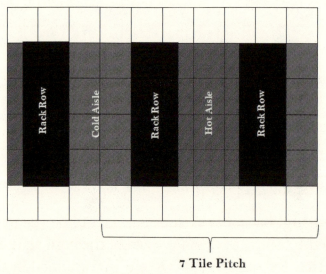

Figure 9: 7 Pitch Tile Rule

COMPONENTS IN THE DATA CENTER

The cooling unit is placed at the hot aisle. Proper distance should be maintained between the air cooling unit and the equipment, typically between 2.5m and 10m.

Sealed Rooms

The data center should be completely sealed to prevent the escape of cold air to the external environment. This could progressively worsen the energy situation as more and more energy is consumed to adequately cool the server room space only for the cold air to escape to other areas.

Airflow Management

Open spaces in the cabinets should be minimized as much as possible. This can be done by placing blanking plates in unused rack unit spaces, blocking of cabinet sides, and making use of perforated front and back doors.

Cable Management

Cables impede airflow in the data center. They must be properly managed and routed to enable cold air to reach its desired destination.

Aisle Containment

An increasingly popular strategy, aisle containment involves the complete demarcation of the cold aisle or hot aisle, so that the cold air, or hot air, is contained in the aisle. This eliminates the inadvertent mixing of cold air with hot air, providing the maximum benefit of the 7 tile pitch arrangement.

It is generally less complex to contain the cold air so that the general environment in the data center becomes hotter while the inlet to the IT equipment becomes a lot colder. If hot air is to be contained, a mechanism to channel the hot air out to the cooling units needs to be installed.

This brings about another complexity. If we contain the cold air and allow hot air to discharge to the environment, how do we cool the room for the workers in the Data Center?

Manufacturers have reacted by designing cooling units to stand in line with the IT racks and cabinets, in the same row. Units like these are generally referred to as In-Row Units.

With the use of In-Row units, the hot air can instead be contained. The In-Row units can then suck in the hot air as it is discharged from the IT equipment. More and more data center designers are favoring this approach.

COMPONENTS IN THE DATA CENTER

Figure 10: In-Row Cooling Unit

CRAC vs CRAH

Most newcomers to Data Centers often confuse the terms CRAC and CRAH. What do they mean?

CRAH is an acronym for Computer Room Air Handler, while CRAC is an acronym for Computer Room Air Conditioner.

CRAHs are indoor cooling units that do not have their own compressors. They are typically components of a Chilled Water system based cooling system.

CRACs on the other hand have their own self-contained compressor. They are a staple of Direct Expansion based cooling systems.

ANCILLARY SYSTEMS

Data center ancillary systems are those systems that are installed to maintain the aesthetics and operational integrity of the data center. These systems are not critical to the operation of the data center but could have a lot to do with the sustainability, maintainability, and long term reliability of the data center.

They include Access Control Systems and CCTV systems for **physical security**, fire detection and suppression for **safety**, Environment/Energy Monitoring Systems (EMS) and Data Center Infrastructure Management Systems (DCIM) for **monitoring and management**, and raised floor, suspended ceilings and cable trays for **cable and airflow management, and data center aesthetics.**

Planning safety and security for the Data Center will be the subject of a future publication.

DATA CENTER STANDARDS

With the advent of the PC in the early 1990s, high computing power suddenly became available with a low footprint. Servers dedicated to specific services immediately followed. The arrival Servers gave birth to the Server Room phenomenon.

As more and more companies built Server Rooms, it became apparent that there was a need to agree on specific standards for the design. Different organizations used to employ different, often haphazard, methods for their specific designs, which more often than not created chaos in the Server Rooms.

Servers have continued to become more powerful, with smaller sizes and higher processing capacities, increasing the ratio of computing power to Server Room space. The effect is the need for more efficient cooling.

The data center is increasingly more important as business and consumption trends rely more and more on data center availability. We now rely fully on Mobile Apps and the Cloud, with increased adoption Remote Learning, Remote Desktop, and Thin Client models. The entirety of activity, processing, storage, and analysis rests in the Data Center.

Standard Bodies

The following are some of the more recognized Data Center bodies:

- The Uptime Institute
- The Telecommunications Industry Association (TIA)
- The Building Industry Consulting Service International Inc. (BICSI)
- The American Society of Heating, Refrigerating and Air-Conditioning Engineers (ASHRAE)

Uptime Institute

The very first and most widely recognized standards body is the Uptime Institute, which came up with the Tier rating system in 1995. They meticulously define that the Tier rating system measures data center design outcomes, differing greatly from other standards, which detail specific checklists that must be followed.

Data Center designs are classified as either Tier I, Tier II, Tier III, or Tier IV, depending on design objectives and outcomes. The highest tier level does not necessarily indicate the best design, rather it is business objectives that determine the best tier level to target.

Details of the Uptime Institute Tier Classification can be seen here:

https://uptimeinstitute.com/tiers

Uptime Institute also provides professional consulting practice and retains the right to certify that data centers have been built to a certain Tier classification. Uptime Institute Tier Certification is a coveted asset for data centers, as it confirms that the data center meets internationally recognizable operational expectancy, which is especially important for data centers looking to attract colocation users.

Details of the Uptime Institute Tier Certification program can be seen here:

https://uptimeinstitute.com/TierCertification

TIA

The Telecommunications Industry Association (TIA) is a body renowned for network cabling standards. Its cabling standards cover Buildings, Campuses, and more recently, Data Centers.

The TIA, in conjunction with the American National Standards Institute (ANSI), created the TIA-942 Data Center Standard in 2005. A revision was issued in 2010, named TIA-942-B.

Initially, the TIA 942 built on Uptime Institute's Tier Classification system, providing additional directives for network cabling topology, power, cooling, monitoring, security, building services, civil works, and many more. However, owing to disagreements over how the standards should be laid out (outcome-based or following a strict set of rules), Uptime Institute retrieved the right to publish their standards from TIA.

TIA-942-B revision is very specific and detailed on its tier rating and the attendant requirements for each level of redundancy and availability.

Details of the TIA 942 standard can be seen here:

https://global.ihs.com/doc_detail.cfm?&csf=TIA&document_name=TIA%2D942&item_s_key=00414811

BICSI

As at the time TIA was working on its Data Center Standard, the Building Industry Consulting Service International Inc. (BICSI) was also working on theirs. The BICSI issued its standard, BICSI 002-2010: Data Center Design and Implementation Best Practices, also in 2010.

In many respects, the BICSI 002-2010 is similar to TIA 942. Many of both passages can be mapped to each other. Only in minute details do both documents disagree.

Also, just as the TIA standard has undergone a revision, BICSI has also updated its standard with a new release: ANSI/BICSI 002-2019, Data Center Design and Implementation Best Practices.

DATA CENTER STANDARDS

The BICSI standard however does not specify a tier rating system. It only details best practices and recommendations as well as references to external organizations' standards, such as those from the American Society of Heating, Refrigerating, and Air-Conditioning Engineers (ASHRAE).

Details of the NSI/BICSI 002-2019 standard can be found here:

https://www.bicsi.org/standards/available-standards-store/single-purchase/ansi-bicsi-002-2019-data-center-design

ASHRAE

The American Society of Heating, Refrigerating and Air-Conditioning Engineers (ASHRAE) is a global society dedicated to advancing the arts and sciences of heating, ventilation, air conditioning, and refrigeration to serve humanity and promote a sustainable world. Founded in 1894, ASHRAE publishes journals, whitepapers, technical resources, and global standards that advance its objective, which is *"to serve humanity by advancing the arts and sciences of heating, ventilation, air conditioning, refrigeration, and their allied fields"*.

ASHRAE publishes and maintains a standard that establishes the minimum energy efficiency requirements for the design and operation of data centers, the ASHRAE 90.4 standard. The current iteration of the standard is the

2019 update, the ANSI/ASHRAE Standard 90.4-2019, Energy Standard for Data Centers.

Standard 90.4 offers a framework for the energy-efficient design of data centers with special consideration to their unique load requirements compared to other buildings. The standard was developed under the guiding principle that data centers are mission-critical facilities demanding careful attention to the potential impact of its requirements.

Details about the standard and requirements for compliance are available here:

https://www.techstreet.com/ashrae/standards/ashrae-90-4-2019?product_id=2092750

NEXT STEPS

The foregoing is a brief overview of what a Data Center is, what it consists of, and what to consider when designing one.

I may have succeeded in quelling your curiosity, and perhaps I only ended up fueling them.

You may decide that a career in Data Centers is what you want to pursue. You may require further development and training.

I would recommend that you proceed to read either or both of these books:

Designing Data Centers – Book 1: Power (Available on Amazon at: www.amazon.com/dp/B08NWBF7SG) which is a detailed discussion on Electrical Power and how it applies to the data center, and

Designing Data Centers – Book 2: Cooling (Available on Amazon at: www.amazon.com/dp/B08W7JNVKW) which is a detailed discussion on Cooling and how it applies to the data center.

Other books are also in the works to take you through the nitty-gritty of designing and operating data centers.

Would you like to get notified as soon as they are released? Join this list: http://eepurl.com/g-ZkNr

You may need some help on a particular project you are working on, or you might just wish to provide some feedback.

Either way, you can send me an email on dcbadru@gmail.com for your Data Center inquiries.

To your success!

B.A. Ayomaya

BIBLIOGRAPHY

Authoritative Dictionary of Standards Terms (7th ed.), IEEE, 2000, ISBN 978-0-7381-2601-2, Std. 100

Avoiding Trap Doors Associated with Purchasing a UPS System" (PDF). Archived from the original (PDF) on 2013-03-26. Retrieved 2018-12-11.

Cotton, Bart (January 2005). *Battery Asset Management: VRLA ageing characteristics* (PDF). Batteries International. Archived from the original (PDF) on 2013-04-06.

Cottuli, Carol (2011), *Comparison of Static and Rotary UPS* (PDF), Schneider Electric, White Paper 92 rev. 2, retrieved April 7, 2012

Fink, Donald G.; Beaty, H. Wayne (1978), *Standard Handbook for Electrical Engineers (11 ed.)*, New York: McGraw-Hill, ISBN 978-0-07-020974-9

Generex. *Multi-XS User Manual* (PDF). Archived from the original (PDF) on 2012-01-27. Retrieved 2011-11-14.

Geng, Hwaiyu (2015). *Data Center Handbook*. Palo Alto, CA: John Wiley & Sons, Inc.

Hayt, William (1989). *Engineering Electromagnetics* (5th ed.). McGraw-Hill. ISBN 0070274061.

High-Availability Power Systems, Part I: UPS Internal Topology (PDF). Emerson Network power White Paper, 2000. Archived from the original (PDF) on 2013-03-26. Retrieved 2018-12-11.

High-Availability Power Systems, Part II: Redundancy Options (PDF). Emerson Network power White Paper, 2000. Archived from the original (PDF) on 2013-03-26. Retrieved 2018-12-11.

Michael F. Hordeski (2005). *Emergency and backup power sources: preparing for blackouts and brownouts.* The Fairmont Press, Inc. ISBN 9780881734850.

Oliver Heaviside (1894). *Electrical papers. 1.* Macmillan and Co. ISBN 978-0-8218-2840-3.

Open Compute Project. Available at http://www.opencompute.org/.

Sawyer R. (2011) *Calculating Total Power Requirements for Data Centers* (PDF), Schneider Electric, White Paper 3 rev. 1, retrieved April 7, 2018.

Solter, W. (2002), *A new international UPS classification by IEC 62040-3*, 24th Annual International Telecommunications Energy Conference, pp. 541–545, doi:10.1109/INTLEC.2002.1048709, ISBN 0-7803-7512-2, S2CID 195862090

Ton, My; Fortenbery, Brian; Tschudi, William (January 2007). *DC Power for Improved Data Center Efficiency* (PDF). Lawrence Berkeley National Laboratory. Archived from the original (PDF) on 2010-10-08.

DESIGNING DATACENTERS
DATA CENTER DESIGN GUIDE
BOOK 1 - POWER

Specifying the requirements, Power Generation, Power Distribution, Power Efficiency, and Fault Tolerance for Data centers

B.A. AYOMAYA

DESIGNING DATACENTERS

Data Center Design Guide
BOOK 1: POWER

Specifying the requirements, power generation, power distribution, power efficiency, and fault tolerance for data centers.

B.A. AYOMAYA

DISCLAIMER

All material used is original work or it has come from public domain sources e.g. the Internet. Should any copyright owner wish to have any items removed, then please contact the author at the following address: dcbadru@gmail.com.

Every effort has been made to provide accurate and complete information. However, the author assumes no responsibility for any direct, indirect, incidental, or consequential damages arising from the use of the information in this document.

Copyright © 2020 Badrudeen Ajibola Ayomaya.

All rights reserved.

No part of this publication may be reproduced, transmitted, transcribed, stored in a retrieval system, or translated into any language or computer language, in any form or by any means; electronic, mechanical, magnetic, chemical, thermal, manual, or otherwise, without the prior consent in writing of the copyright owner. Applications for the copyright owner's permission to reproduce any part of this publication should be sent to the copyright owner by email at the following address: **dcbadru@gmail.com**.

The book is sold subject to the condition that it shall not by way of trade, or otherwise, be lent, re-sold, hired out, or otherwise circulated without the copyright owner's prior consent in writing in any form of binding or cover other than in which it is published and without a similar condition including this condition being imposed on the subsequent purchaser.

"It is not the critic who counts; not the man who points out how the strong man stumbles, or where the doer of deeds could have done them better. The credit belongs to the man who is actually in the arena, whose face is marred by dust and sweat and blood; who strives valiantly; who errs, who comes short again and again, because there is no effort without error and shortcoming; but who does actually strive to do the deeds; who knows great enthusiasms, the great devotions; who spends himself in a worthy cause; who at the best knows in the end the triumph of high achievement, and who at the worst, if he fails, at least fails while daring greatly, so that his place shall never be with those cold and timid souls who neither know victory nor defeat."

- Theodore Roosevelt

CONTENTS

CONTENTS v
Welcome to This Guide ix
INTRODUCTION 1
   What is Power? 3
   Understanding Power – A Primer 4
      Voltage 4
      Current 6
      Resistance 7
      Ohm's Law 9
      Alternating Current (AC) and Direct Current (DC) 10
      Power 15
      DC in the Data Center 19
      Electrical Loads 21
      Critical and Non-critical Load 27
POWER SOURCES 29
   Utility 29
   Engine Generators 31
   Renewable Energy Sources 34
   Uninterruptible Power Supply (UPS) 41
      Static UPS 41
      Online Double conversion UPS 44

    Online Delta conversion UPS 45

    Rotary UPS 51

  Hybrid Systems 54

POWER DISTRIBUTION 56

  Surge Protection Device (SPD) 56

  Voltage Regulators 57

  Isolation Switches 58

  Transfer Switches 62

  Switchgears 64

  Power Distribution Units 67

  Plugs and Sockets 68

  Cables and Wires 70

  Earthing, Grounding and Bonding 74

  Power Distribution Topology 78

DETERMINING THE NEED 86

  The Concept of N 86

  Calculating N 88

    UPS Sizing 89

    Cooling Loads 90

    Generator Sizing 91

    Path Elements Sizing 93

  Redundancy 95

  Tier Specification 96

ENERGY EFFICIENCY 100
  The Need for Energy Efficiency 100
  Energy Efficiency Metrics 103
    Power Usage Effectiveness 103
    Data Center Infrastructure Efficiency 107
    Data Center Energy Productivity 111
    Energy Reuse Effectiveness 113
    Carbon Usage Effectiveness 116
  Energy Efficiency Certification Standards 119
    LEED 119
    BREEAM 120
    ENERGY STAR 121
  Energy Efficiency Best Practices 123
    Virtualization 123
    Decommissioning Unused Equipment 124
    Storage Management 124
    Energy-efficient Equipment 125

CODES AND STANDARDS 127
  Uptime Institute 127
  TIA 128
  BICSI 129
  ASHRAE 130
  NFPA 131

CENELEC	132
IET	133
BSI	133
IEC	134
TEN-STEP FRAMEWORK	**136**
The Ten Steps	136
Case Study	141
NEXT STEPS	**142**
BIBLIOGRAPHY	**143**

Welcome to This Guide

If you are reading these words, it means you are interested in designing Data Centers. I welcome you to a rich trove of information.

Perhaps you have come here after reading my first guide – **Data Center for Beginners: A beginner's guide towards understanding Data Center Design**[1]**,** and have decided to master the art of Data Center Design. Or you may be a newbie perching on this nest by chance. You may even be an experienced Data Center professional wishing to sharpen your craft. Regardless, you will find the information contained herein quite useful.

This guide is dedicated to studying the nitty-gritty of designing Power for the Data Center. I have attempted a direct approach devoid of flowery equivocation, aimed at giving you a firm foundation in your Data Center design career.

As an industry veteran, this is the guide I needed when I first started. I trust you will share the same sentiment as well.

I hope it proves to be a valuable companion as you take your career to the next level.

Sincerely yours
B. A. Ayomaya

---

[1] Available on Amazon in Kindle and Paperback editions.

CHAPTER ONE
INTRODUCTION

In today's connected world, businesses more than ever need to, and are, relying on technology to achieve their objectives. The need for IT permeates the entire fabric of the modern enterprise. The way businesses produce, distribute, communicate, support, and deliver goods and services to their internal and external customers is heavily reliant on IT. This profound dependence predicates the importance of the Data Center.

The Data Center exists to enable the business' IT needs. Businesses realize their IT needs by running applications on Servers, saving data on Storage, and sharing information through Networks. These IT building blocks are set up and operated on in the Data Center.

The most critical aspect of the Data Center is Power. Power accounts for up to 40% of the Data Center requirements. Power is the foundation upon which all other Data Center components are built. Without power, even the most sophisticated IT installations come to naught. Facility Managers will testify to how frequent the outages of IT systems are blamed on the loss of power.

The above is to underscore how important the understanding of Power and all its aspects - generation, distribution, and delivery – is to you, the budding Data

Center designer. The subsequent pages will help you on this journey.

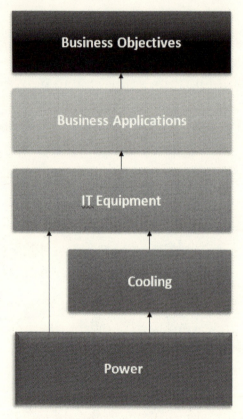

The Data Center Value

What is Power?

The word "Power" connotes different meanings depending on the context it is used. In our context, we are referring to electrical power.

Electrical power is the rate, per time, at which electrical energy is transferred by an electrical circuit.

Refer back to Chemistry. We learn from the Law of Conservation of Energy, that energy cannot be created or destroyed in an isolated system, but can be transformed from one form to another.

The other forms of energy include Nuclear Energy, Chemical Energy, Mechanical Energy, Thermal Energy, Radiant Energy, and Sound Energy. Electrical energy is generated by transforming one of the other forms of energy through the use of special equipment. These special equipment are collectively called the Electrical Power Plant.

Electrical Energy by itself is useless to the IT Equipment. It needs to flow through a path. This path is called an electrical circuit. When electrical energy is transferred from one point to another through an electrical circuit, the rate, per time, at which this transference occurs is called electrical power, measured in Watts (W).

Equipment manufacturers specify the number of watts required for that equipment to function, or *power-up*.

Electrical power is the rate, per time, at which electrical energy is transferred by an electrical circuit.

Understanding Power – A Primer

Understanding electrical power will require familiarization with some concepts. I will assume that you, the reader, already have some knowledge of the basic physics of electricity. This section will help refresh your memory at a high level. It might still be helpful though to consult other sources if necessary.

Recall from Physics that we have electricity when electrical charges are able to flow continuously through a medium, known as the conductor. When conductors are connected in such a way that charges are able to flow in a closed, endless loop, we have an electrical circuit.

We can control and manipulate the movement of charges, and ultimately power, by understanding these three concepts – Voltage, Current, and Resistance.

Voltage

For electric charges to move to form electricity, there must be a push from somewhere to cause this movement to happen. The pressure, or tension, that causes the charges to move from one point to another is called Voltage. Voltage is the difference in potential energy between two points that will cause a unit charge to move from one of the points to the other. The charges move from the point with higher potential energy to that with lower potential energy. By definition, Voltage is the work required to move a unit charge between two points. Voltage is measured in Volts (V) and is represented in equations by the letter V.

Voltage, also known as Electric Potential Difference, is the work needed per unit of charge to move a test charge between the two points.

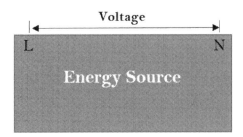

The 'L' terminal has a higher potential than the 'N' terminal. This difference in potential, the Voltage, will move the charge from the 'L' to the 'N' terminal if a continuous path exists between both terminals. That path is created by connecting a material that welcomes the flow of charge through it, technically called a Conductor, to both terminals. The standard conductor used in practical applications is Copper, and the continuous path is called a Circuit.

If there is a break in the continuous path, the charges will not be able to reach the 'N' terminal and the circuit is said to be Open. When the break is remedied and continuity is restored, the circuit is said to be Closed.

Current

We have learned that charges move around in a circuit from the point with higher potential to the point with lower potential. The flow of the charge, or the rate per time at which the charge moves around in the circuit, is known as Current.

Electric current is the rate of flow of electric charge

Current is measured in Amperes (A) and is represented in equations by the letter I.

Current only flows in a closed circuit. If a circuit is open, current will not flow.

Consider the illustration below.

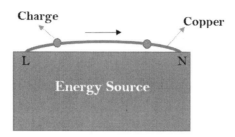

Copper links the 'L' to the 'N' terminal to form a closed circuit so that current will flow. However, this type of circuit in technical parlance is called a Short Circuit, and is potentially dangerous.

Because copper is such a good conductor, a high amount of current flows through the circuit, delivering a large amount of energy back to the Energy Source in a short period of time. This causes a rapid rise in temperature that can damage components and potentially cause an explosion.

Short circuits are avoided by reducing the amount of charge that flows through the conductor thus limiting the current flow in the circuit. The concept of resistance helps in achieving this.

Resistance

When current flows through a conductor, not all the charge that originally gets on the conductor finds its way to the end of the path. This is because materials have an inherent property that opposes the flow of current through them. This property is called Resistance.

Resistance is the opposition to the flow of current in an electrical circuit

Resistance is measured in Ohms (Ω) and is represented in equations by the letter R.

Conductors have a low resistance, which is why current flows easily through them. Other good conductors after copper are silver, gold, and aluminum, but it is not economically sensible to dedicate these elements to just current flow.

Materials with high resistance so that they restrict the flow of current are known as Insulators. Examples are rubber, glass, and wood.

Because the inherent resistance in a conductor is low, another component, called a Resistor, is introduced in the circuit to provide the required resistance to control the amount of current flowing through the circuit. This is especially required if there other components in the circuit that are averse to the limitless flow of current.

Ohm's Law

We have seen what Voltage, Current, and Resistance mean. We can also see that these phenomena are closely related.

There can be no current if we do not have voltage. The higher the voltage, the higher the current flowing through the circuit. On the other hand, if there is high resistance in the circuit, low current flows, regardless of the amount of voltage present.

This relationship can be explained empirically by Ohm's Law. The Law was formulated and named after a German scientist called Georg Simon (1784-1854). Ohm's Law is expressed in the mathematical formula:

$$V = I \times R$$

Where

V = Voltage in volts,

I = Current in amps, and

R = Resistance in ohms

With this formula, the value of one of measures can be determined if the value of the two other measures are known. We can rewrite the formula thus:

$$I = \frac{V}{R}$$

or

$$R = \frac{V}{I}$$

If we examine a circuit and discover that there is infinite resistance, we are sure that there will be no current. And if we find an infinite flow of current, we know that there is zero resistance.

If we find that there is current as well as resistance, we can know what the voltage must be. And if we know the voltage and the current, we can determine the resistance.

Voltage, current, and resistance in a circuit can be measured using applicable electric meters.

Alternating Current (AC) and Direct Current (DC)

In practical applications, you would discover that the types of current you encounter are not homogenous. The characteristics of the current from the voltage source will most times differ from that seen on the on-board circuitry of the data center IT equipment.

There are two types of current. In **Alternating Current (AC)**, the direction at which the electrical charges flow change periodically. In **Direct Current (DC)**, the electrical charge flow maintains a single direction.

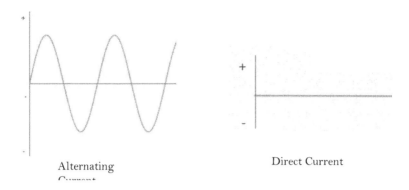

Alternating Current

Direct Current

This difference in charge flow direction is due to the way the Current is being generated. We will discuss more on this in the appropriate section.

AC can be converted to DC and vice-versa. A device that converts AC to DC is called a **rectifier**, while a device that converts DC to AC is called an **inverter.**

Inverters convert DC to AC. Rectifiers convert AC to DC.

The form in which current is delivered to homes and offices is mostly AC. It is AC we consume when we plug our appliances to power outlets on the wall.

We consume DC when we use batteries to directly power equipment. Batteries produce DC from chemical reactions that happen within it.

Most digital electronics like PCs and mobile devices use DC. Any device that makes use of an adapter for power is most likely using DC, as is the case with PCs and mobile devices.

Data center devices like servers and switches usually have inbuilt adapters to convert AC from the power source to DC before it being introduced to the internal board circuitry.

AC Characteristics

Due to the constant directional changes in AC flow, several characteristics have come to be defined to describe the quality of the AC. Some of these characteristics include:

Waveform, which describes the pattern of voltage oscillation in AC. Examples are Sine Wave, Square Wave, and Triangle Wave.

Amplitude, which is the maximum value of voltage or current when current flows from rest in a single direction. It can be positive or negative. Positive indicates current flowing upwards from rest (0), and negative indicates current flowing downwards from rest (0).

Peak, which is the point at which current flow reverses direction.

Cycle, which is one complete repetition of the wave pattern.

Frequency, which is the number of cycles in a sine waveform per second, measured in Hertz (Hz).

Alternation, which is one half of a cycle.

Period, which is the time it takes to complete one cycle.

Peak to Peak, which is the voltage difference between the positive and negative amplitudes. It is twice the amplitude.

Root Mean Square (RMS), which is the actual usable voltage. It is derived by dividing the maximum amplitude by the square root of 2. RMS could refer to voltage or current.

$$RMS\ Voltage = \frac{Peak\ Voltage}{\sqrt{2}}$$

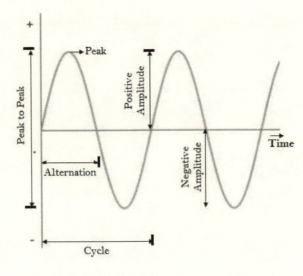

Sine Wave Characteristics

A/C Phase

In practical applications, there may be a need to produce multiple unsynchronized voltages. These voltages are usually produced at the same frequency so that even though the waveforms have the same amplitude, they do not reach their peak at the same time. This is called a **phase shift.** The phase shift is described in terms of degrees. The phase that is ahead is said to be *leading*, while the one behind is said to be *lagging*.

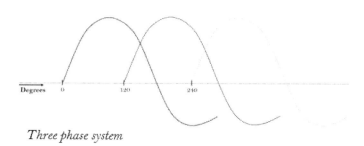

Three phase system

Consider the sine waveforms above. The waveforms can be said to be 120 degrees out of phase with each other. The Red phase leads the blue phase, while the yellow phase lags the blue phase.

We will discuss further on how multiple voltages are generated in a later section.

For simple applications, a single phase is usually sufficient. However, three phases are common in industrial applications. Homes and offices can have one, two, or all three phases delivered.

Power

Previously, we have established that *Power* is the rate at which electrical energy is transferred in a circuit. Since *Current* describes the charge flow through a circuit, it follows that electrical energy is transferred as a direct result of the flow of current.

If this is the case, does there exist an equation to show this relationship? As a matter of fact, there is.

INTRODUCTION

James Joules (1818 – 1889), an English scientist, discovered what is now known as Joule's first law in 1841, which he describes as follows:

"...the heat which is evolved by the proper action of any voltaic current is proportional to the square of the intensity of that current, multiplied by the resistance to conduction which it experiences".

In other words, the Power present in a conductor as a result of current flowing in it can be described with the following equation:

$$P = I^2 \times R$$

Or,

$$P = I \times V$$

Since,

$$R = \frac{V}{I}$$

Where,

V = Voltage in volts,

I = Current in amps,

R = Resistance in ohms, and

P = Power

With this formula, we can determine the conductor size required to deliver Power to an equipment. When we know the power requirement of that equipment as stated by the manufacturer, and we know voltage delivered from the voltage source, we can then calculate the amount of current that must flow through the circuit and size the cabling accordingly.

In a three-phase circuit, the equation is slightly different. The power to the equipment is delivered from the current flow in each of the lines. Power usage can be computed by measuring the voltage and current flowing through each line, using the following formula:

$$P = I \times V \times \sqrt{3}$$

Where,

    P = Power delivered to equipment

    I = Current measured in the phase line

    V = Voltage measured in the phase line

Reviewing both Ohm's and Joule's Laws reveals differing relationships between current and voltage.

INTRODUCTION

From Ohm's Law, current is directly proportional to voltage, so that more voltage generates more current if resistance is held constant,

$$I = \frac{V}{R}$$

While from Joule's Law, current is inversely proportional to voltage, so that a higher voltage indicates lower current if power is held constant.

$$I = \frac{P}{V}$$

Is this not a contradiction?

There is no inconsistency. This is because Ohm's Law deals with the *beginning* of electricity generation, and Joule's Law deals with the *end*.

Ohm's Law lets you know that if you increase the voltage present in the circuit, and you do not increase the resistance to charge movement, more current will flow as a result.

Joule's Law shows that if you want the same amount of power in the circuit for use by your equipment after increasing the voltage, you must necessarily reduce the current flow by increasing the resistance present in the circuit. If you do not do so, more current will flow, leading to more power and possible damage to your equipment. Ohm's Law is always obeyed.

Ohm's Law describes the relationship between voltage and current *with respect to* resistance, while Joule's Law describes the relationship between voltage and current when you have to keep power constant.

DC in the Data Center

If most data center equipment use DC, then why distribute AC to the data center. Why not just deliver and use DC instead? Here is why.

Power from the grid is meant to be delivered for use by equipment in homes, buildings and data centers. This means a lot of power. The government also needs to minimize the costs of delivery, including loss of energy to heat. Even if power is generated in the data center, the power needs to be delivered for use in different spaces and facilities, with attendant heat losses.

The heat loss can be calculated from Joule's Law:

$$H = I^2 R$$

It follows that there are two ways to reduce heat loss, either reducing the current or reducing the resistance inherent in the conductor i.e. using thicker cables.

Using bulkier cables will cost more, and will strain the suspension towers due to the heavier weight. This leaves us with the option of reducing current.

We know that,

$$P = IV$$

If we can somehow manipulate the voltage generated such that it increases and current reduces by the same rate, we will still get the same power. Then the heat loss due to distribution will also reduce by the square of that rate!

Luckily, AC allows voltage amplified as well as reduced. A device that converts voltage from high to low and vice versa is called a **transformer**. With the aid of transformers, power can be transmitted at very high voltage and at low current from the generating source. The voltage can then be stepped down at designated demarcation points to acceptable values for onward power distribution to the data center load.

We cannot play this trick with DC. Hence the industry has settled on using AC for distribution.

This was not always the case. You can read up on the so-called "War of Currents" in the 1800s between Thomas

Edison and the George Westinghouse backed Nikola Tesla.

The fittest survive the test of time, and there can be no better indicator of fitness than efficiency. AC power plants are much more efficient, and AC-based distribution ultimately prevailed.

Electrical Loads

Electrical loads are the objects in an electric circuit that consume the power being delivered to the circuit. They are the objects plugged into the power outlets.

There are three types of electrical loads: Resistive Loads, Inductive Loads, and Capacitive Loads.

Resistive Loads as the name implies resists the flow of current through it by immediately converting the energy delivered to a useful form, such as heat or light. As a result of the immediate usage, the voltage and current waveforms are completely in phase.

Resistive loads loosely map to heating loads such as incandescent lights, ovens, heaters, etc.

Inductive Loads are loads that need to power electric motors for them to operate. The rotation of the motor creates a magnetic field which takes time to develop after voltage is applied. As a result, the current waveform lags the voltage waveform. This phenomenon is called inductance.

Inductance is the property of an electric conductor or circuit that causes an electromotive force to be generated by a change in the current flowing.

Inductive loads loosely correspond to mechanical loads. They are load with moving parts. Examples are fans, compressors, washing machines, vacuum cleaners, etc.

Capacitive Loads are loads that store the energy being delivered in the circuit and then release the energy back in the direction of the original energy source. This phenomenon is known as capacitance.

Capacitance is the ability of a system to store an electrical charge.

There are no actual standalone objects that are purely capacitive. Instead, you find it in capacitors present in a circuit.

As a result of the phase difference between the voltage and the current in inductive and capacitive loads, a secondary power is generated in the circuit. This power, in technical parlance, is referred to as *reactive power*.

The actual power from the energy source delivered in the circuit is referred to as *apparent power*, while the power that is actually used to do work is referred to as *true power*.

Reactive Power is measured in reactive volt-ampere (VAR). Apparent Power is measured in volt-ampere (VA), while True Power is measured in watts (W).

What concerns us as designers is to have as much True Power as possible.

When a circuit has inductive or capacitive loads, some of the apparent power is lost in the form of reactive power, so that true power is always less than apparent power.

In inductive loads, the reactive power is in the direction of the apparent power. In capacitive loads, the polarity is reversed. The reactive power here is directed back at the energy source.

Consider the figures below.

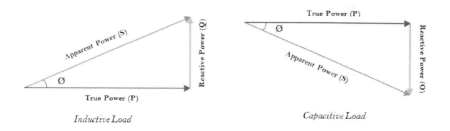

Inductive Load   *Capacitive Load*

With inductive load, reactive power pushes up apparent power at an angle ø, which is the phase difference between voltage and current. Reactive power has a positive value as it is consumed by the load. Voltage leads current.

With capacitive loads, reactive power has a negative value as it is supplied back to the energy source. Here, voltage lags current.

Drawing from our knowledge of mathematics, the magnitude of the apparent power can be calculated thus:

$$|S|^2 = P^2 + Q^2$$

Therefore,

$$|S| = \sqrt{P^2 + Q^2}$$

Where,

S = Apparent Power (VA)

P = True Power (W)

Q = Reactive Power (VAR)

The **Power Factor (PF)** is the measure of how efficient a circuit is. It is the percentage of apparent power that contributes to the true power. It can be computed by taking the cosine of the phase angle between the voltage and the current.

$$PF = \cos\emptyset = \frac{P}{S}$$

Where,

    PF = Power Factor

    S = Apparent Power

    P = True Power

    Ø = Phase Angle between Current and Voltage

The closer the power factor is to 1.0, the more efficient the circuit is. Facilities with low power factor are usually susceptible to penalties from the utility provider, because power that could be useful elsewhere is being supplied, yet is not actually used to do work.

Power factor can be corrected in a circuit. With reactive power induced by inductive loads, a network of capacitors is added to the circuit so that the reactive power needed by the inductive loads are provided by the capacitors. Thus the total apparent power demanded will reduce, lowering the phase angle Ø and bring the power factor closer to unity. Another way is to try to minimize inductive loads in the first place.

Capacitive loads are only used to control power in the circuit as in power factor correction and are rarely standalone loads.

Powering the Load

Recall from our earlier discussion on voltage and current that current flows from the terminal that has a higher potential, normally designated as 'L', to the terminal with a lower potential, designated as the 'N' terminal. To facilitate the flow of current, a conductor connects the 'L' terminal for the power source to the 'L' terminal of the load and likewise for the 'N' terminal. This allows the flow of charges to the load via the 'L' line where they are used to power the load. Remnants, if any, flow through the 'N' line to the power source.

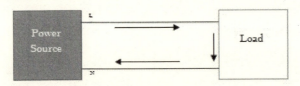

Single Phase Power Flow

This is why physically touching the 'L' line will electrocute a person while touching the 'N' line will not, provided there is a continuous connection on both the 'L' and 'N' lines between the power source and the load. In electrical terminology, 'L' means Live, while 'N' means Neutral.

For three phase systems, current flows along all three lines. Each line is then branched off to power different loads. It is important to ensure that balance is maintained in the power drawn from each of the lines.

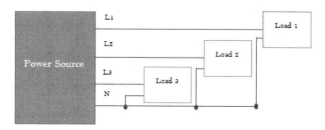

Three Phase Power Flow

Critical and Non-critical Load

In the Data Center, electrical loads can be classified into two: critical loads and non-critical loads.

Critical loads are the IT equipment for which the data center exists, as well as the equipment that support the operation of the IT equipment.

Non-critical loads are those that, if removed or isolated, do not have any impact on the operation of the critical equipment.

Consider a data center with two servers, a network switch, a cooling unit, an access-controlled door, and a fire protection device. All of these are electrical loads. However, only the two servers, the network switch, and the cooling unit are critical loads. The access control and fire protection devices are non-critical loads.

The servers and the network switch are the devices whose operation required the data center in the first place. The cooling unit is required to maintain temperature conditions optimal for the servers and switch operation. Without it, the servers and switch would shut down, thus rendering the entire data center inconsequential.

The access control and fire protection, although important, do not directly affect the operation of the critical equipment. Removing them will only impact the safety and security of the environment. Without any fires or sabotage, the data center will still provide the outcomes for which it was designed.

However, if there is some sort of automated sequence of operation triggered by non-critical loads that affect the critical loads, the non-critical loads become critical. For example, if the detection of fire will cause fire protection to power off the cooling unit, the fire protection device becomes a critical load.

CHAPTER TWO
POWER SOURCES

From the foregoing, we now have a fair understanding of what Power is. We also have a fair understanding of important concepts related to Power. Our attention now turns to sources from which Data Centers get their Power, concentrating on Alternating Current sources.

Utility

Utility is a collective term used to describe power generated by external parties and supplied to the data center to be consumed at an agreed tariff between the data center operators and the external generating parties.

Utility can be from the electrical power grid operated by the government. It can also be from electrical service companies.

Utility is usually generated at high voltage and low current, so that smaller conductors are used to distribute power over long distances. Upon arrival at the data center, the power is transformed to a lower voltage and higher current, using bulkier cables to transmit power over shorter distances.

POWER SOURCES

Power from the grid can be generated and transmitted at up to 200kV before it is stepped down to 11kV (Europe and Africa) or 4kV (US) for distribution to the data center.

Another transformer is typically present in the data center facility to step down to nominal acceptable supply voltages in the facility. Depending on the location, nominal supply voltages can range between 100V – 240V for single phase systems, and 240V to 400V for three phase systems.

Power Transformer (ABB)

As Utility is not controlled by the data center, loss of power from Utility cannot be predicted or prevented. This makes Utility an unreliable source of power to the data center, so that data center operators are moved to generate their own power for use by the facility.

Engine Generators

Data centers primarily generate power through Engine generators. Engine generators are devices that convert mechanical energy into electrical energy primarily through the principle of electromagnetic induction.

Promulgated by Michael Faraday in the 19th century, electromagnetic induction implies that when there is relative motion between a coiled conductor and a magnetic field, an electric current is induced to flow in the conductor.

There are two ways the electricity is induced in production. Either there is a fixed magnetic field with the coil constantly rotating in the field, or the coil is wound around a magnet and the magnet is constantly rotated. The former is more common.

The coil rotates in a clockwise direction. As the coil rotates, the direction of current flow alternates between the positive and the negative thus producing an alternating current.

The component of the engine generator that produces the AC current is known as the **alternator**. Below is a simplified diagram of an alternator.

POWER SOURCES

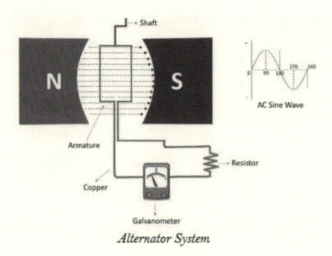

Alternator System

The armature is a loop of wire rotating in a magnetic field. The shaft is used to continuously rotate the armature. The shaft is activated through other electrical or mechanical means.

The galvanometer is used to detect the presence of current and observe the direction of current flow. The resistor in the circuit is to reduce to current flow to amounts tolerable by the galvanometer.

When the armature rotates 90º, the current flow reaches its peak as seen in the AC Sine Wave graph. As it rotates to 180º, the current flow diminishes until it reaches zero. When the second half cycle commences, the current flows in the opposite direction until it reaches its peak, then diminishes back to zero.

Thus, a complete cycle of rotation gives the AC sine wave with characteristics described in the previous section.

The other mechanical components in the engine generator ensure that the shaft keeps rotating the armature.

An engine-generator is rated by the quantity of power the alternator generates. As described above, the power factor of the engine generator determines the actual quantity of power available downstream. The apparent power generated is measured in kVA, while the true power available to the Load is measured in kW. Thus, a 500kVA engine generator with a power factor of 0.8 has an apparent power capacity of 500kVA and an actual supply capacity of 400kW.

Engine generator power is rated in one of three types: Standby Power Rating, Prime Power Rating, and Continuous Power Rating.

Standby Power Rated engine generators are not designed to be the primary source of power. These generators are meant to be used to supply power in emergency situations for a limited period until the primary power sources can be restored. This is the most common application of engine generator sets.

Prime Power Rated engine generators are able to supply power for extended periods. The Prime Power indicates the maximum capacity of the engine generator.

Engine generators should not run at 100% of the prime-rated capacity for more than 500 hours per year. However, if the generator is the primary source of power to the facility, the total load should not exceed 70% of the prime rating[2], except otherwise stated by the engine generator manufacturer.

Continuous Power Rating indicates that the engine generator can be loaded at 100% capacity for an unlimited length of time. This is applies to data centers where the primary source of power is the engine generator.

The elevation and temperature of the engine generator location have an effect on the engine operation and thus the power capacity. At an elevation above 1000m and a temperature of about 40°C, the power capacity is usually de-rated. Actual elevation and temperature limits, and de-rating percentages, are specified by the engine generator manufacturer.

Renewable Energy Sources

Traditional engine-generators use fossil fuels to drive the mechanical components that ultimately rotate the shaft in the alternator. Fuel is a substance that can be

---

[2] See the ISO 8528-1 specification

made to react with other substances to release energy that is used for work, or to provide heat.

Fossil fuels are formed by natural processes and contain a high percentage of carbon. Using fossil fuels typically releases harmful gases such as CO_2 to the atmosphere. As data centers consume a large chunk of power generated, there is a drive to consider other generation methods, or fuel sources, that do not have adverse effects on the environment.

Renewable energy sources are those sources that are sustainable and always available in nature. Fossil fuels are not renewable as they are finite. If the current store of fossil fuel is exhausted, we will not be able to get more during our lifetime. Renewable sources, however, like sunlight and wind, are infinite.

Another benefit of renewable energy is that they do not release negative by-products and gases that characterize fossil fuels.

Nonetheless, traditional techniques still dominate the power generation sector. This is because it is quite expensive to harness the power in the large quantities required from renewable energy sources.

The most common renewable energy sources are Solar Energy, Wind Energy, Hydro Energy, Geothermal Energy, and Biomass Energy.

Solar Energy is harnessed from the light and heat emanating from the Sun. It is estimated that the solar energy delivered to the earth's surface in one hour is sufficient for our requirements for a whole year.

Solar energy is converted to electrical energy through a process known as the *"photovoltaic effect"*. Solar panels are positioned to capture as much sunlight as possible. The solar panel is an enclosed layer of silicon cells with wiring to allow for the flow of current. When the silicon cells absorb sunlight, the current begins to flow. This current is in the form of Direct Current, so an inverter is placed in its path to convert the Direct Current to an Alternating Current form for use by the equipment in the facility.

Some of the DC is stored in batteries for use at a time when sunlight is low or unavailable.

Solar Panel

Electricity can also be generated by harnessing enough heat from sunlight for use by a thermal power plant. Mirrors or lenses are carefully aligned to focus enough sunlight to heat an object up to 2000OC. This heat can be used to activate a boiler, which then generates the needed steam for a steam turbine generator plant.

A thermal power plant converts heat energy to mechanical energy, which is then employed by the alternator to generate electricity.

Wind Energy is energy from the wind. The force of the wind is used to rotate the blades of a wind turbine around a rotor, which is then used to spin the armature in a nearby connected AC generator.

A wind turbine is a device that converts kinetic energy from the wind into electricity. The wind turbine blades are made of very light and resistant materials to allow for ease of movement, even with light winds. The turbine also detects very strong winds and adjusts its spin rate to control generated voltages. The turbine blades are coupled to a shaft which is connected to an electricity generator to provide the rotation necessary for AC generation.

Wind Turbine

Hydro Energy is energy from the movement of water. Large quantities of water are collected in a dam or reservoir at a higher elevation. The water is then released in a controlled fashion to fall on a turbine, causing it to rotate. The rotating turbine is used to drive generators, thus generating electricity.

Hydro Energy is the most widely adopted and commercially developed renewable energy source. In 2019, it accounted for up to 18% of the world's power generation capacity.

An advantage it has over solar and wind energy is that the flow of water can be controlled to produce electricity at the rate of demand. During off-peak periods, the extra power can be used to pump water back to the elevated position, to be released again during peak periods. Solar and wind energy supply cannot be manipulated and is left to the devices of nature. For this reason, solar and wind energy is deemed unreliable.

Hydro Energy can also be harnessed from the tidal current from nearby shores. Tidal current is the horizontal movement of water accompanying the rise and fall of ocean tides. Tides are said to be one of the most reliable phenomena in nature. Thus tidal current is highly predictable. The tidal current is used to drive the turbine and generate electricity.

Geothermal Energy is energy from the heat below the earth's surface. The deeper we go beneath the earth's surface, the hotter it becomes. It is estimated that the temperature of the earth's inner core, the innermost part of the earth, is as hot as the surface of the sun!

Geothermal energy is not evenly distributed around the earth. Geothermal energy is highest in places that have lots of hot springs and volcanic activity because the earth is quite hot just below the surface at these locations.

Electricity is generated from geothermal energy through geothermal power plants. Wells are dug deep into the earth to pump steam to the surface. The steam is used to power a steam turbine for the rotary motion used by the generator to generate electricity.

Biomass Energy is energy from biomass, which are renewable organic materials from plants or animals. Examples of biomass include wood, crops and animal manure.

Biomass can be burned to directly provide heat energy for domestic and industrial use. Biomass can also undergo thermal, chemical, or biological conversion to product solid, liquid and gaseous fuels. Fuel from biomass is called biofuel.

Biofuel differs from fossil fuel in that it is produced through fast contemporary processes, as against the extremely slow geological process through which fossil fuel is formed.

Biofuel is considered renewable as the plant and animal sources can be renewed through farming.

Biofuel is used to produce electricity similar to the way fossil fuels are used. Burning biomass and biofuel also releases gases that pollute the atmosphere.

An alternative to combustion is the use of fuel cells.

A fuel cell is a device that converts the chemical energy of a fuel and an oxidizing agent into electrical energy and heat energy via clean chemical reactions. As there is no generator in this process, Direct Current is produced.

Thus, using biofuel with fuel cells has the potential for producing clean, renewable and reliable electricity in appreciable amounts for use in the data center facility.

Uninterruptible Power Supply (UPS)

Uninterruptible Power Supply (UPS) systems are not technically power generation systems. However, UPS is an important capacity component in the data center.

The UPS seats between the generator and the load. When there is an outage from the generator, the UPS provides emergency power until power from the generator can be restored.

In addition to providing backup power, the UPS also corrects anomalies inherent in supplied power from the generator. These include fluctuations in supply voltage and frequency.

UPS can be divided into two broad categories, Static and Rotary, based on the manner backup power is provided to the load.

Static UPS

Static UPS is the most common implementation of UPS systems. They are so named because they do not have any moving parts throughout the power flow.

This type of UPS provides emergency power by converting DC stored in a battery to AC for onward supply to the load.

We know that an *inverter* converts AC to DC, and a *rectifier* converts DC to AC. Therefore, a UPS has an inverter and a rectifier as part of its internal components.

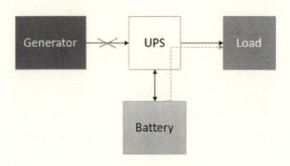

When power from the generator is restored, the UPS converts AC from the generator into DC to be stored in the battery.

There are several configurations through which power could be routed to the Load and the battery. This leads to further sub-categorization as follows:

- Offline UPS
- Line Interactive UPS
- Online Double Conversion UPS
- Online Delta Conversion UPS

Offline UPS

Here, the Load is powered directly from the mains when the mains input is present. The UPS switches the load over to the battery when the mains input goes off.

There is a noticeable time lag during the switching process. More so, the irregularities (if any) in the mains power are carried over to the Load. These make this configuration not conducive for sensitive critical Load.

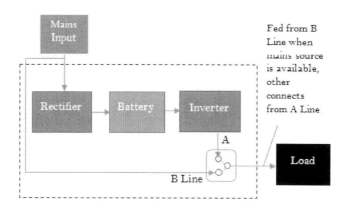

Line Interactive

This configuration is similar to the Offline system. However, a voltage regulator is introduced after the mains just before the Load.

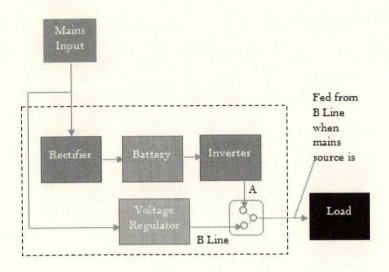

The Voltage Regulator corrects some of the irregularities, but cannot correct frequency. There is still a noticeable time lag during the switching process. Critical Load is not to be powered with this system.

Online Double conversion UPS

This configuration completely isolates the Load from the mains input. The Load is always fed from the DC Power.

The AC power from the mains is converted to DC to keep the batteries charged. The inverter then converts the DC back to AC to supply the Load.

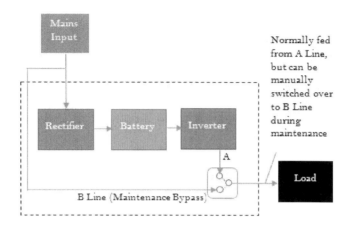

This ensures that the supply to the Load is always clean and continuous, making it suitable to critical Data Center Loads. A bypass is included so that the Load can be switched manually switched over to the mains supply temporarily during maintenance operations.

One drawback however is that this configuration is not very efficient due to losses accrued during the conversion processes.

Online Delta conversion UPS

This is a variation of Line-Interactive system. It uses a Delta Converter in place of the Voltage Regulator. The Delta Conversion UPS allows a portion of the Load to be fed from the mains, while the rest is fed from the

Inverter. This allows the stabilization of the output voltage. It also ensures that there is no switching time lag if the mains input is cut, as the Inverter can seamlessly assume the rest of the Load.

This configuration provides the greatest efficiency. However, frequency anomalies cannot be corrected.

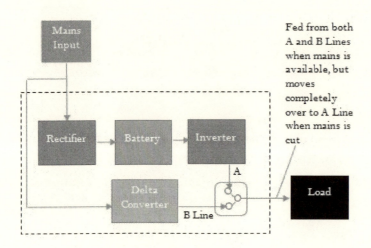

Batteries

We have seen that the UPS stores DC in batteries. But how does the battery hold the DC and stop the charges from flowing away?

Batteries store electrical energy in the form of chemical energy. A battery is typically a collection of *cells* lumped together to produce greater output capacity. Each cell is made up of three main components: a positive terminal, a negative terminal, and an electrolyte. The electrolyte is a chemical substance that can be easily decomposed by chemical reactions.

The positive and negative terminals are conductors but are of different materials. If they are made of the same material, charges will not flow.

In batteries, charges flow out from the negative terminal and return through the positive terminal.

When the load is connected to the battery, chemical reactions take place within the battery that disintegrates the electrolyte freeing electric charges and ions. The released charges then flow through the circuit to the load. Since there is no alternation, the charges flow in a single direction giving Direct Current (DC).

When all of the charges from the disintegrated electrolyte flow out, current stops flowing, and the battery is said to be flat.

Recharging the batteries actually works by reversing this sequence. Charges that flow into the positive terminal from the recharge source recombines with the floating ions to reform the electrolyte. However, the electrolyte cannot be fully restored to the same capacity it was prior to discharge so that the battery eventually becomes permanently flat.

Some types of batteries cannot be recharged. These batteries are generally called dry-cell batteries as the electrolyte is usually in powdery form. They have the advantage of lasting for much longer than it would take a rechargeable battery of the same size to fully discharge. However, they don't find much use in the data center.

Most traditional data center UPS applications use Valve Regulated Lead Acid (VRLA) batteries, which is a variation of Lead Acid batteries. These use lead-based terminals and sulphuric acid as the electrolyte.

When Lead Acid batteries are recharged, some of the hydrogen gas hitherto freed from the chemical reactions are released before being able to recombine to reform the electrolyte. Likewise, some of the electrolytes are lost to leakage and spillage.

VRLA batteries solve this by sealing the electrolyte inside the container and immobilizing the electrolyte thus simultaneously trapping released hydrogen gas and preventing electrolyte movement and leakage. However, if the internal pressure during recharge builds up too much or the gases are released too quickly before they can recombine, a valve is automatically opened to free some of the pent up gas. The immobilization of the electrolyte ensures that none can be lost to spillage when the valve opens.

VRLA Battery

The electrolyte immobilization is done either by containing thin fiberglass mats between the plates as is the case with **Absorbent Glass Mat (AGM)** battery, or by mixing with silica dust to take a gel-like form, as is the case with **Gel Cell** battery.

VRLA batteries however have a disadvantage. There is a limit to the depth to which they can be discharged, and the number of times they can be recharged. They also are typically heavy. VRLA batteries have a maximum shelf-life of 10 years, although due to environmental factors they tend to be replaced every five years.

A fast-growing alternative to VRLA batteries is Lithium-ion (Li-on) batteries. Typically found in cell phones and laptop computers, Lithium-ion batteries are increasingly used to backup UPS systems in modern data centers.

Li-on batteries typically are up to 50% lighter than VRLA batteries of similar capacities. Although they discharge quicker than VRLA batteries, Li-on batteries can be discharged more deeply and recharged more often than their VRLA counterparts. Li-on batteries also have a life expectancy of more than 10 years and provide a more environmentally friendly option when they eventually have to be disposed of. They are not without disadvantages though. Li-ion batteries will explode if they're dangerously overcharged or if an internal malfunction causes a short circuit. Manufacturers find different ways to mitigate this shortcoming, although the concern remains.

Battery Capacity

The battery capacity, which is the length of time in which the battery can supply an average amount of current to the load before falling flat, is measured in AH (Amps × Hours).

The voltage resulting from the chemical reactions in the battery cell is usually 2V. Batteries with a higher voltage have several individual cells connected in series. A battery described as 12V 200AH would typically have six 2V cells connecting in series and having a combined capacity of 200AH.

As the battery is discharged, the battery voltage decreases. To compensate for this decrease, more current will be drawn. The battery becomes flat when the voltage falls below a manufacturer's specified threshold.

This is called the *cut-off voltage*. If the battery is further discharged beyond the cut-off voltage, permanent damage is done and the battery cannot be recharged anymore.

A battery with a 200AH capacity supplying an average of 2 Amps current to the load will in theory last for 100 hours at the set battery voltage.

However, the room temperature where the battery is stored, and the way the battery is discharged, affects the battery lifespan, so that expected runtime may not be applicable. It is important to follow manufacturer guidelines when deploying batteries.

How long should batteries last?

Since the UPS is only meant to provide placeholder power until power from the generator is restored, batteries are usually designed to provide backup power for about 15 minutes. This provides sufficient time to return generator power.

Rotary UPS

Like the Static UPS, Rotary UPS stores energy so that it can provide emergency power to the load in the event of outages from the main source. However, while the Static UPS stores energy in the chemical form in batteries,

POWER SOURCES

Rotary UPS stores energy in the kinetic form in a flywheel.

A flywheel is a mechanical object specially designed to efficiently store kinetic energy usually in the form of a spinning wheel, or disc, or rotor, rotating around its symmetry axis.

When a rotational force is applied to the flywheel, it starts to spin at increasing speed until it reaches the maximum allowable rotational speed. When the rotational force, or torque, ceases to be applied, the flywheel gradually loses its momentum until it stops spinning.

In a Rotary UPS, the flywheel is used to drive the rotational movement of the alternator in an AC generator. The torque is provided by power from the main source. When a power outage occurs, the momentum of the flywheel keeps the alternator for a short while until the power is restored. Rotary UPS usually has a ride-through time of about 15 seconds. Some implementations incorporate batteries to extend the backup time.

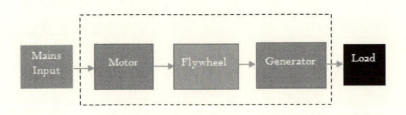

In other implementations, the Rotary UPS is attached to a diesel engine. This is known as the Diesel Rotary Uninterruptible Power Supply device (DRUPS). A reactor or choke coil filters out power quality problems from the mains before reaching the flywheel. When an outage occurs, after a set delay, the diesel engine is started and takes over from, or works concurrently with, the flywheel to power the load. The delay is set so that the diesel engine is not started at every incident to prevent wear and tear.

Rotary UPS systems are usually manufactured for higher power ranges (200kW and above). DRUPS systems are generally not found in capacities lower than 500kW.

As a result of the relatively short ride-through time, DRUPS systems require a rigorous maintenance regime to ensure that it remains reliable when called upon. It has a lot of moving parts, hence is easily prone to failure. Yet, it has the advantage of having a much low Total Cost of Ownership (TCO) compared to Static UPS. It has a smaller footprint, is more efficient, and can withstand warmer ambient temperatures, making it suitable for practical applications especially when the required power capacity for the critical load is very large. It also has a considerable lifespan compared to its Static UPS counterpart.

POWER SOURCES

DRUPS (Hitachi Hirel)

Hybrid Systems

The power generating sources we have looked at all have prominent roles in data center deployments. Each has its advantages and demerits, in terms of cost, availability, sustainability, and maintainability. But what if we could combine different power sources in such a way as to derive the cumulative advantages?

The obvious potential does not escape manufacturers. Several equipment makers have debuted products that promise to maximize the power economy. Some of these products have a combination of solar panels with storage in lithium-ion batteries and fuel cells or diesel generators, together with an intelligent power switching system. The switching system determines which of the sources to activate in such a way as to maximize savings.

For instance, if the load is not much and there is enough sun, the load could be powered entirely from the solar component. If an additional load is added and the battery is fully charged, battery capacity can be added to support the load. If the sun begins to set and the battery bank is considerably discharged, the generator can be started. If the load is shed and the battery is fully charged, the generator can be put off and the load runs on battery. If utility is available but the solar component can support in its entirety, utility cost can be saved by running on solar.

Intelligent decisions on how to mix, match, and switch the sources can have real savings on the Total Cost of Ownership (TCO) of the data center power system.

The above was a discussion on the ways power can be generated to support data center critical load. Collectively they are referred to as **power capacity components**. We will now turn our attention to the way generated power is delivered to the data center equipment.

CHAPTER THREE
POWER DISTRIBUTION

Different elements feature along the power distribution path to the data center critical load. Collectively, they are referred to as **path elements.** We will examine those commonly found in data center power systems.

Surge Protection Device (SPD)

A surge protection device is a device that protects critical equipment from damage in the event of a power surge. Anomalies may occur that trigger a surge in the voltage and current flowing through the circuit. Since the on-board circuitry of critical equipment is rated for a set power, a surge can easily cause a lot of damage to the electronics.

Some causes of surge can be frequent turning-on and turning-off of capacity components, lightning strikes, and electro-magnetic disturbances to power cables. Lightning strikes in particular cause significant damage, as they could cause voltage surges as high as 50,000V.

Surge Protection Device

Surge protection devices take the excess power flowing through the circuit and channels it along an alternative path away from the critical equipment. Surge protection devices are typically placed just after the capacity components in the circuit.

Voltage Regulators

The voltage from power generating equipment may sometimes be irregular. It may be too low, too high, or frequently fluctuate. A voltage regulator manages the voltage from the capacity component and keeps it within limits acceptable to the load.

Automatic Voltage Regulator (Ortea)

Placing a UPS after a generating source usually removes the need for a voltage regulator, as the output voltage is kept constant. However, the UPS itself has limits on the range of voltage acceptable as input. Where generated voltages cannot be controlled, it is advisable to place a voltage generator before the UPS input.

Isolation Switches

Isolation switches are devices that break and make the flow of current in a circuit. When required, they are used to prevent the flow of current further downstream to the load. Some of the more common isolators include circuit breakers, gear switches, relay switches, and contactors.

Circuit Breakers

A circuit breaker is an isolation switch that is originally designed to protect the circuit from damage caused by a short circuit or an excess current flow in the circuit. When such an error is detected, the circuit breaker is tripped automatically and current flow is cut off. The breaker can also be operated manually to prevent the flow of current when required, for instance, during equipment maintenance or installation works.

The type of circuit breaker used depends on the current flowing through the circuit and the power system. In single-phase systems, the breaker can be used to isolate only the 'L' line, as is the case in a single-pole breaker, or both the 'L' and 'N' lines, as is the case in a two-pole breaker. In a three-phase system, a three-pole breaker is used to isolate only the 'L' lines. A four-pole breaker can also be used to isolate all the lines.

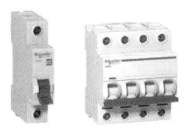

Circuit Breakers (Schneider Electric)

The circuit voltage also determines the type of breaker used, with Low Voltage (0 – 1kV), Medium Voltage (1kV – 72kV), and High Voltage (72kV and higher) all requiring specific types of breakers.

Disconnectors

Similar to circuit breakers, disconnectors isolate current from flowing downstream. Unlike circuit breakers, however, disconnectors are manually operated and do not react to circuit errors like circuit breakers.

Disconnector (Eaton)

Relays and Contactors

Relay switches are typically used in applications where some level of automation is required. Relay switches make or break the circuit in response to some external stimulus.

A relay could be said to be Normally Open (NO) or Normally Closed (NC). When the relay is NO, the contacts are connected so that the current does not flow except the external stimulus is triggered. When the relay is NC, current flows through the contacts by default until the external stimulus is triggered.

A contactor is a switch that is controlled electrically. Similar to relays, contactors also mostly appear in automation applications.

In contrast to relays, contactors are usually directly connected to high current loads. A low current circuit controls the switching of the high current contacts. The controlling circuit is almost always Normally Open.

Relay (Schneider Electric)   *Contactor (Schneider Electric)*

A low voltage source, say 24V, is connected to the Normally Open contacts. In response to an externally monitored occurrence, the contacts can be automatically closed allowing the low current to reach the circuit, so that the higher voltage switch, say 230V, is activated to power the load.

Transfer Switches

A transfer switch is an electrical switch used to transfer the powering of a load from one source to another, for instance, from the generator to utility and vice-versa. The transfer can be manually operated, or automatically activated. An automatically activated transfer switch is called an Automatic Transfer Switch, or ATS for short.

In addition to automatically switching power sources, some Automatic Transfer Switches can send signals to other sources to come online. A common scenario in data center applications is when both utility and generator are available to power the load. Assuming the utility is suddenly interrupted, the ATS can send a signal to the generator to start. Once it determines that the generator has started with acceptable parameters, the load can be shifted to the generator. When utility is restored, similar checks are performed before the load is then returned to be powered from utility. It goes without saying that the data center load is powered from a UPS during the switchover sequences.

Automatic transfer switches have two main modes of operations: Break-Before-Make, where the load is disengaged from one source before being transferred to the other source, and Make-Before-Break, where the second source is connected to the circuit is parallel to the first source before the first source is disconnected. Most ATS operation is break-before-make, especially when the second source needs to be brought online before the switchover is performed. Make-before-break applications are for loads that cannot accept even the slightest loss of power. In such a situation, both sources are always online awaiting switchover when required.

Automatic Transfer Switch (ASCO)

Automatic transfer switches usually make use of mechanical parts to perform load switchover. Transfer switches without any moving parts are called Static Transfer Switches (STS).

An STS is fully electronic, with power semiconductors such as Silicon-Controlled Rectifiers (SCR) used to transfer the load. Without any mechanical moving parts, the switchover is achieved rapidly without cutting off current flow to the load. The load switchover is usually performed in less than a quarter of the power cycle.

POWER DISTRIBUTION

Static Transfer Switch (Vertiv)

Some manufacturers use the term ATS and STS interchangeably, especially when the in rack-mount transfer switches. It is therefore important to study the device specifications before selection for use.

Switchgears

A switchgear, or electrical panel, is a collection of electrical components, conductors, circuit breakers, relays, etc, used to manage the distribution of current to the load in a facility. Instead of directly wiring all the load the power source, switchgears are used to control this flow so that different sections of the load can be isolated for maintenance, repair, or upgrades without affecting the other load sections.

Consider a facility with two floors. The operators want a scenario where one floor can be isolated independent of the other floor.

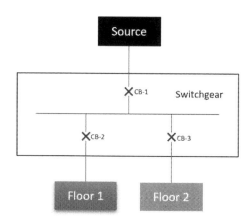

This simple switchgear comprises three circuit breakers and a conductor bus. The circuit breaker CB-1 can be used to isolate the power from the main source from reaching downstream. Circuit breakers CB-2 and CB-3 will isolate only Floor 1 and Floor 2 respectively. It goes without saying that CB-1 will be rated at a higher capacity than both CB-2 and CB-3. In this switchgear, CB-1 is the integral or main circuit breaker. This is because all current downstream, regardless of distribution topology, can be isolated from this one breaker.

Switchgears can be much more complex depending on the application, power design, and position along the power flow. Switchgears positioned just after the utility or power generators are termed Medium Voltage (MV) Switchgears/Panels. MV Switchgears usually incorporate fault detection and control components, including surge protectors, relays, contactors, transfer switches, meters, and circuit breakers. Switchgears positioned for further distribution downstream are termed Low Voltage (LV) Switchgears/Panels.

BlokSet Switchgear (Schneider Electric)

LV Panels can also be used for control applications, power factor correction, or simple power distribution.

Power Distribution Units

Power Distribution Units are used to distribute power to the load. They are usually positioned after the UPS in the power flow. Power distribution units can be wall-mounted LV switchgears, stand-alone floor standing units, or rack-mounted power strips.

Power distribution units can be basic, metered, switched, or metered and switched.

Basic PDUs contain only simple components without any instrumentation or management capability.

Metered PDUs contain electrical meters to display the load running on each line.

Switched PDUs contain components that enable individual receptacles to be switched on or off remotely.

Metered and Switched PDUs contain both electrical meters to display running load and remote switching components.

Switched and Metered Rack Mount Power Strip

Since basic PDUs are not monitorable, it is very easy to overload circuit and erroneously trip circuit breakers. It is also a major culprit in phase unbalancing. It is better to invest in at least a metered PDU for a better-managed power system.

Plugs and Sockets

With power finally distributed to the equipment racks, we need to find a way for the equipment to access the power. Instead of wiring directly, we make use of plugs.

Plugs are used to connect the equipment to the power source. One end of an appropriately sized conductor is connected to the equipment internal circuitry while the other end is connected to a plug. The power source, typically a rack-mount power strip, will have a socket where the plug will enter.

IEC C13 Plug

IEC C13 Socket

Plugs allow equipment to be easily isolated for maintenance, repair, or upgrade. With plugs, any work to be done on a single piece of equipment would not require a circuit breaker controlling the power feed to the rack to be switched off. The equipment's plug is simply removed.

Rack-mount power strips themselves usually have plugs. Cabling from the upstream switchgear or PDU is typically terminated with a socket. The corresponding plug is terminated on the rack-mount power strip so that it can be easily isolated without turning off the upstream source.

32A, 230V Rack-mount Strip Plug

Plugs come in various sizes and form-factors, governed by various standards. *Some* of the well-known bodies that define standards for plugs and sockets are the International Electrotechnical Commission (IEC) and the US-based National Electrical Manufacturers Association (NEMA). It is therefore important to ensure compatibility between the plugs used by the equipment and the outlet in which the plugs are to be inserted.

Cables and Wires

We know that current flows from one point to another through conductors. We also know that materials that resist the flow of current are called insulators. Touching a bare conductor will cause the current flowing through to branch through our bodies, causing electrocution.

In order to safely install conductors to carry current from the generating station to the equipment needing the power, an insulating material needs to be wrapped around the conductor. Such a material, a piece of conductor inside an insulating sheath, is called a wire.

An electrical cable is a group of wires bundled together inside a common sheathing called the cable jacket. Cables are used to deliver power to electrical equipment.

For an equipment to access power, a continuous path needs to exist between it and the generating station through which current can flow. Current flows from the generating source to the equipment and back to the generating source.

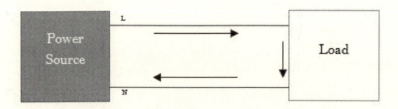

To achieve this, multiple wires need to be run to Power Source terminals to the Load terminals. For efficiency, cables are used. The cables can then contain the required number of wires bundled together and run at once.

Wires are typically cylindrical. The most common conductor used in a wire is copper, though aluminum appears in some installations.

The conductor in the wire can be solid and hard. This allows for ease of installation and termination, and lower resistance. However, the wire becomes difficult to bend and twist. This kind of wire is called a *Solid Wire*.

The conductor can also flexible with strands twisted together. This allows for easy manipulation especially when the cable path contains many twists and bends. A Wire with flexible conductor strands is a *Flexible Wire*.

Wires are usually described by their cross-sectional area. A wire with a 1.5mm² cross-sectional area is called a 1.5mm wire. That with a 2.5mm² cross-sectional area is called a 2.5mm wire. And so on.

Describing cables also incorporates the number of wires. For instance, a cable bundling three wires each with a 1.5mm² cross-sectional area is called a 1.5mm by 3 core cable. A cable with four wires each with cross-sectional areas of 2.5mm² is described as a 2.5mm by 4 core cable. And so on.

Wires are also measured by the diameter width. Another widely used non-metric gauge is the American Wire Gauge (AWG). Increasing AWG numbers a decrease in the wire diameters.

The bigger the wire cross-sectional area, the less the resistance and more current is able to pass through. Wires need to be sized appropriately to allow the expected flow of current, else they overheat and possibly catch fire.

Cables are available in production in different sizes, shapes, wire types, and outer coverings. Choosing a cable type for your application depends on several factors e.g. cable route, fire protection, ease of installation, etc.

When the cable route is along a path where it can be damaged outer exertions, it is important to have another protective layer over the wires. A common cable type used for this scenario is the Armored Cable. A metallic sheath, mostly steel, is placed over the wires to protect against any physical damage.

The material sheathing the cable wires, the cable jacket, is a potential source of fuel for fires. When cables are to be laid in areas where a fire outbreak would be difficult to control, for instance indoors, one must pay close attention to the cable jacket material. The jackets could be made of fire-resistant material or coated with fire-retarding substances so that any fire outbreak can be abated before fire extinguishing action.

Cables can be distributed to the power equipment overhead so that it drops down to the equipment from the top, or underground, so it rises up to the equipment from under. Different kinds of cable trays, hangers, and distribution accessories exist to manage this distribution.

Earthing, Grounding and Bonding

When an electrical surge occurs, or other unwanted charges are hanging around, we need to find a way to divert the charges away from our equipment so they do not cause unwanted damage. Fortunately, the bare earth is a near bottomless sink for charges. It can absorb as many charges as available. It is therefore critical to create a path through which the unwanted charges in the electrical system can be diverted to the bare earth. This is called grounding.

Grounding is the connection of a conductor between an electrical circuit and the bare earth so that excess charges can flow to the earth.

There are several ways through which unwanted charges can be generated. When a conductor carries current, the conductor radiates an electromagnetic field. Through electromagnetic induction, a conductor around the radiated electromagnetic field can pick up energy, leading to undesired transmission. Likewise, when there is an electrical surge, unwanted charges are transmitted.

Because the internal circuitry of electrical equipment contains conductors, the unwanted charges can be transmitted to the internal circuit thereby damaging the equipment.

Electrical cables carrying current usually have a dedicated earth cable to protect the equipment. Unwanted charges can be diverted to the dedicated earth wire so that they can be channeled to the earth. Therefore, a single-phase system typically uses a three-wire cable, while a three-phase system uses a five-wire cable.

Three Wire Cable   Five Wire Cable

A widely used colour code for earth cables is yellow with green stripes. The earth wires across the installation must be properly connected to the main grounding circuit of the facility. This process is called Earthing.

Earthing is the connection of the exposed conductive parts of an installation to the main grounding terminals of that installation. Sometimes earthing and grounding are used interchangeably since they both imply connecting the exposed conductive parts to the earth.

In a data center facility, some electrical conductors are not part of the electrical system. They are not meant to carry any current. This includes exposed metallic surfaces of equipment racks, switchgears and other building structures, service pipes and ducts, metallic protection sheath over cables, lightning protection system, etc. However, since they are conductors, it is possible that charges accidentally land on them, and current will flow. Therefore, in the data center facility, every conductor not used for current-carrying must be connected to the grounding circuit. Connecting to the grounding circuit ensures that any unwanted charge picked up by the conductor is channeled to the earth.

In an electrical installation, it is important to ensure that all non-current carrying conductors have equal electric potentials with reference to the earth. In other words, the measured voltage between a non-current carrying conductor and the earth should be the same for every non-current carrying conductor.

Why is this important? Suppose you are standing between two racks, and both racks have different electric potentials. If you were to touch one rack with one hand and another rack with the other hand, you have created a circuit between both racks because you are a conductor. Now, current always flows from the point of higher potential to the point of lower potential. If an electrical charge were to land on the surface of the rack with a higher potential, it will flow through you to the other rack, and you could be electrocuted. However, if both racks were to be of the same potential, the charge will remain, and if the rack is grounded, will flow to the earth. Therefore, we need to ensure that all extraneous conductors have the same electrical potential, which should also be the same as the main building grounding system. This process is called equipotential bonding.

Equipotential bonding is the electrical connection putting various exposed conductive parts and extraneous conductive parts at substantially equal potential. We do this by having a direct conductor connection between the extraneous conductive surfaces and the main ground system of the building.

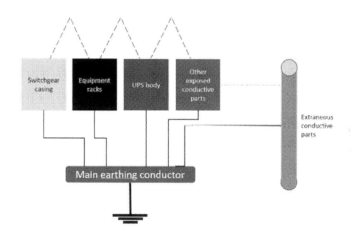

Equipotential bonding

Appropriately sized cables directly connect the exposed conductive parts of the installation and other extraneous conductive parts to the main earthing terminal. This terminal is then wired directly to be buried underground.

Conductors can optionally connect the conductive parts for complementary equipotential bonding.

Grounding and subsequent equipotential bonding is vital for the safety of data center equipment as well as maintaining a safe working environment in the data center.

Power Distribution Topology

We have seen the common elements that appear in the delivery path of power to the equipment in the data center. We will now examine how they are arranged along the path.

Consider the block diagram below.

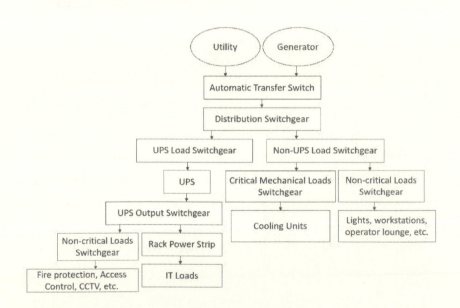

Electrical Schematic

The above is a simple illustration of the power flow in a data center. The data center takes supply from the utility company. However, it also has a backup generator if utility supply is interrupted. Both the utility and generator are connected to an Automatic Transfer Switch (ATS) to spontaneously power on the backup generator and migrate the load to it when utility is interrupted. If utility is restored, the ATS will test the power quality and confirm stability, then migrate the load to utility and power off the generator.

An appropriately sized cable connects the ATS to a switchgear to distribute power to the rest of the data center.

We have a UPS switchgear through which power reaches the UPS and, subsequently, the IT loads and other non-critical loads that need the backup provided by the UPS.

We have another switchgear that distributes power the mechanical loads that are not on the UPS as well as the other non-critical loads.

All the switchgears provide a means of isolating power flow from the upstream sources as well as to individual equipment. The switchgears can also be metered so that we can read the total power consumption of loads being fed from each switchgear.

The critical loads and non-critical loads have unique switchgears. This is to enable complete isolation of the non-critical loads without any possible effect or impact on the critical loads.

There are no redundancies to any of the capacity components or path elements in this configuration.

The electrical system of a data center can have different configurations and combinations of capacity components and path elements. There is no standard topology that all data centers must follow. The designer needs to consider the specific requirements of the data center, which is determined by:

a) The business need
b) Operational sustainability

In today's digitally driven world, a data center running mission-critical applications cannot afford any downtime due to the loss of a single path element, hence the simple arrangement above is not sufficient. Suppose the utility goes off and the generator fails to start for whatever reason, what happens next? What if the ATS is damaged? What if the UPS becomes faulty? What if any of the cables feeding any of the critical switchgears gets broken unintentionally? What if a breaker in the switchgear trips off? What if an operator mistakenly unplugs a power strip? There are too many things that can go wrong.

Adding redundant capacity components, or redundant path elements, or both, can significantly impact the required initial expenditure outlay but will safeguard against considerable revenue losses over the lifetime of the data center.

However, for an office where the data center serves only internal users and short downtimes can be accommodated, single capacity components and path elements might be appropriate.

The unique scenario of the data center dictates the design decisions.

Suppose the business needs require redundancy in capacity components. We can have a design topology as follows:

POWER DISTRIBUTION

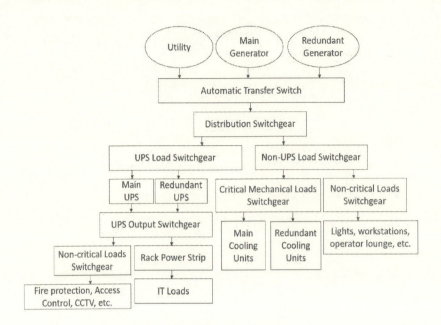

Redundant capacity components

The above is a topology with redundant capacity components. If the main generator is faulty, the redundant generator can be started to power the load. The same thing holds for the UPS and cooling units. There are redundant equipment to provide cover for the main equipment.

For configurations such as this, a rigorous maintenance regime needs to be in place to ensure that the redundant capacity components will run when they are required to support the load.

However, should there be any need to isolate any of the path elements, such as maintenance works, part repairs, replacements, or upgrades, the entire IT Load will be impacted. To avoid this, we can design for redundant capacity components and path elements.

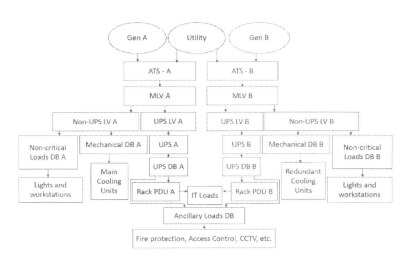

Redundant capacity components and

The above is a topology of two systems, A and B, each redundant to the other in serving the critical loads. For every generator, ATS, MLV Switchgear, LV Switchgear, Cooling Unit, and Power Distribution Unit in System A, there is a similar redundant component in System B. This ensures that power gets to the IT loads through two separate and distinct power paths.

The non-critical loads do not have that luxury. Some of the lights and workstations are powered from System A, while others are powered from System B.

Although it appears that the fire protection, access control, CCTV, etc, have two distinct feeds, power reaches them from just the Ancillary Loads DB. If this switchgear is faulty, they do not get power. The two power paths thus collapse into one path.

While the data center designer may be tempted to embed as much redundancy as possible, one must keep in mind that implementing such a design is very expensive. Components and resources will be fully paid for, yet they will only be sparsely used. That is not an efficient utilization of resources. Beyond initial expenditure outlay, operation costs will continue to run. The equipment will need to be maintained, fuel tanks will need to be refilled, and batteries will need to be replaced. All these will have a significant impact on the bottom-line.

However, having redundant capacity components, and path elements, will give the confidence that the data center can be operated without any loss of power.

The designer should carefully weigh the decision on the right topology to follow against the actual business needs, the losses that might accrue due to down-time, the reliability of the equipment to be deployed, and the availability of efficient maintenance systems.

Nevertheless, the designer should err on the side of caution. The data center is a long-term investment and business needs can change very quickly. IT resources that may be deemed tolerant of downtime may suddenly become highly critical. The data center power system must be designed in a way that is flexible and malleable to cater for the different evolutions of the business needs.

CHAPTER FOUR
DETERMINING THE NEED

The Concept of N

In many data center conversations, the concept of 'N' is a recurring feature, so much so that it may bring some confusion.

The N concept in data center parlance simply means Need. As the data center comprises of multifaceted fields of expertise, usage of the term "N" depends on the particular context. In the electrical system, "N" can be used in the context of **capacity**, or in the **context** of quantity.

In the context of capacity, "N" implies the total power that needs to be generated from the capacity components for all the electrical loads intended to run in the data center, critical or non-critical, to be powered effectively. All the elements along the path to the load need to be sized accordingly as well.

The data center designer needs to determine N for engine generator capacity, N for UPS capacity, N for circuit breaker sizes, N for cable sizes, and N for every other capacity component and path element that needs to operate for the data center to fulfill its objective effectively.

In the context of quantity, "N" implies the quantity of capacity components that need to be combined to provide the capacity required to power the data center loads.

Suppose a Data Center is to be constructed to host a total of 60 racks. The operators wish to load an average capacity of 4kW on each rack. Therefore, the total capacity required in the data hall would be 240kW. In the context of the data hall capacity, N = 240kW.

N capacity in the data hall has to be provided from a UPS system. Obviously, in addition to the N capacity in the data hall, the total UPS output has to consider, UPS distribution losses, UPS battery charging, heat losses, etc. Assuming these additional loads come up to 50kW, in the context of UPS system capacity, N = 290kW.

Now, if the UPS systems procured by the operators each have a capacity of 30kW, they would require ten units to achieve the required UPS capacity. In this case, in the context of UPS quantities, N = 10.

Recall that the cooling capacity components as well have to be powered. Suppose the entire mechanical plant requires 250kW to be powered. In addition, other non-critical loads like ancillary systems are to be powered as well, requiring up to 50kW. The UPS systems need to be supported as well. All this power will be provided by the engine-generator sets.

From our scenario, the engine-generator sets must collectively provide a minimum of 600kW continuous output, to cater to the UPS systems, mechanical plant, non-critical loads, and distribution losses. Therefore, in the context of engine-generator system capacity, N = 600kW.

If the maximum capacity generator that can be purchased is 300kW, in the context of generator quantities, N = 2.

As is seen from the above scenario, N could refer to any number of this. Therefore, when conceptualizing "N", one needs to clearly specify what context it is to be used.

Calculating N

The starting point of every data center design endeavor is to determine N, in the context capacity, required to deliver the business objectives.

Sizing the electrical system for a data center requires an understanding of the amount of power required by primarily the critical IT loads, the ancillary loads protecting them, the cooling system supporting them, the UPS system providing backup power, and the power losses that may accrue from distributing generated power to these loads. A needs assessment is carried out to these requirements.

As long as the power needs of the IT loads can be determined, the power requirements of the other elements can be estimated with relative accuracy using some simple rules. These rules have been arrived by observing relationships in many data centers.

UPS Sizing

Power system designers need to size UPS systems accurately. Unforeseen capacity needs may force power outages when capacity upgrades need to be carried out. Care must be taken as well to not overestimate the needs leading to expensive initial expenditure, and ongoing maintenance expenditure outlays.

The following need to be considered when sizing UPS systems:

IT Loads. These are the primary loads to be supported by the UPS. They are the equipment that deliver the actual value the business hopes for from its data center investments.

Ancillary Loads. These are additional loads required for maintaining an optimal environment for the operation of the IT Loads e.g. lights, security systems, safety systems, etc. Not all ancillary loads need to be on UPS. For instance, most designers put only a few emergency lights on UPS.

UPS Battery Charging. When the UPS battery is fully or partially discharged, recharging draws significant power. This can rise to up to 20% of the UPS capacity, but the actual charging power differs from one product to another.

UPS Efficiency Losses. In a typical installation, UPS efficiency is around 88%. Like battery charging power, UPS efficiency varies between UPS product models. For most products, UPS efficiency also depends on the loading percentage of the UPS.

Power Distribution Losses. As current traverses the power path, some of the electrical energy is lost to heat. Though negligible, the UPS sizing needs to account for this.

The total load on the UPS should not exceed 80% of the UPS capacity. After determining the UPS size, the designer needs to estimate the power needs of other critical data center components to appropriately size engine generator capacity.

Cooling Loads

Cooling systems are inductive loads. This implies that on start-up, they draw power that exceeds that drawn during steady operation.

There are different types of cooling technologies, but we can broadly categorize them into chilled water systems and direct expansion systems. As a rule of thumb, chilled water systems consume about 70% of the total electrical load, while direct expansion systems require about 100% of the total load.

Generator Sizing

It is important that the choice of generator selection should be based on the kW rating, not kVA rating. The kVA rating is the *apparent power* supply output. The kW rating is the *true power* supply output after considering the power factor.

The generator should be able to supply the required capacity for an unlimited length of time. As a rule of thumb, the engine generator loading should not exceed 70% of its stated kW capacity.

The worksheet below can be used to estimate the power requirements:

DETERMINING THE NEED

S/N	Item	Calculation
	Power requirement for Electrical Loads	
1	IT Loads	nameplate kW rating
2	Ancillary Loads	#1 * 0.05
3	Total steady state critical load power draw	(#1 + #2) * 1.05
4	UPS inefficiency and battery charging	(#1 + #2) * 0.32
5	Total power to support to electrical demands	#3 + #4 +#5
	UPS Size Estimate	
6	UPS Sizing	#6 * 1.25
	Power requirement for Electrical Loads	
7	Total power to support cooling demands (Chilled Water Systems)	#6 * 0.7
	Power requirement for Electrical Loads	
8	Generator Sizing	(#6 + #8) * 1.5

Path Elements Sizing

After the required power is generated, it needs to be delivered in sufficient quantities to the electrical load. Current flows through the circuit along the path elements until it reaches the critical load. It follows that each path element needs to be sized to allow the right amount of current to flow through it.

Recall Joule's Law as discussed in the previous chapters. In single-phase systems,

$$I = \frac{P}{V}$$

and in three-phase systems,

$$I = \frac{P}{V \times \sqrt{3}}$$

where,

    P = Power

    I = Current

    V = Voltage

DETERMINING THE NEED

Consider the diagram below

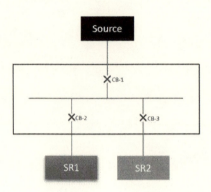

SR1 and SR2 are equipment racks while CB-1, CB-2, and CB-3 are circuit breakers.

Assume SR1 and SR2 hold only single-phase equipment, and both require 3kW (3000W) at a voltage of 230V to power the equipment. The required current flow to each rack is computed as follows:

$$Current = \frac{3000}{230} = 13.04$$

Hence both CB-2 and CB-3 should be sized at slightly above 13.04A, say 16A. Likewise, the cables connecting CB-2 to SR1 and CB-3 to SR2 should have enough thickness for 16A of current to flow through.

The upstream source must generate the 6kW (6000W) needed by both SR1 and SR2 so that CB-1 must allow 26.1A of current to flow through it. CB-1 is thus rated at slightly higher than 26.1A, say 32A. The cables connecting the upstream source to CB-1, and CB-1 to the circuit bus, should have enough thickness to allow 32A of current to flow through.

Path elements at sized at a rating slightly higher than the expected current flow to allow for the distribution losses before the current gets to the load.

Redundancy

So many redundancy expressions exist in literature. The most common examples are N + 1, 2N, and 2(N+1). These expressions refer to N in the context of quantities needed to deliver required capacities.

N + 1 describes a system with N quantities of capacity components, and an extra component with the same capacity as those providing the N capacity.

2N describes a situation where there are two separate systems, System A and System B, each providing N capacity from N components.

2(N + 1) describes a situation where there are two separate systems, System A and System B, each consisting of N + 1 capacity components.

Tier Specification

Originally defined by the Uptime Institute, the tier specification classifies data centers with regard to their complexity and in-built redundancies.

There are four data center tiers.

Tier I – Basic Capacity

A data center designed for Tier I only has the basic required capacity components and path elements, without any redundancy.

Any planned or unplanned disruptions for maintenance, repairs, or upgrades will necessitate the complete shutdown of the data center until the activity is completed.

Tier I data centers have an expected uptime of 99.671% (28.8 hours of downtime annually).

Tier II – Redundant Capacity

A data center designed for Tier II only has redundancy in all the capacity components. However, there is no redundancy in the power path. Only the basic required path elements are present.

Any planned activity on the capacity components may not require a shutdown of the entire facility. However, unplanned disruptions will result in a shutdown. Planned or unplanned interruptions to path elements will shut down the facility.

Tier II data centers have an expected uptime of 99.741% (22 hours of downtime annually).

Tier III – Concurrently Maintainable

A data center designed for Tier III has redundancy in all the capacity components. It also has redundant paths through which power can get to the critical equipment. All the redundant paths do not need to be active at the same time.

Any planned activity on the capacity components does not require a shutdown of the entire facility. Likewise, works on any path element do not necessitate an outage. Power can simply be diverted to the other paths. Unplanned activities however may result in an outage.

A Tier III data center with proper operational processes can function without shutting down throughout its lifetime.

Tier III data centers have an expected uptime of 99.982% (1.6 hours of downtime annually).

Tier IV – Fault Tolerant

Like the Tier III data center, a Tier IV data center also has redundancy in capacity components and path elements, with at least two power paths always active.

The complementary capacity components and power paths are physically compartmentalized from each other. Planned and unplanned interruptions will not hamper the data center operation. There is an autonomous response to failure.

Tier III data centers have an expected uptime of 99.995% (26.3 minutes of downtime annually).

The decision on which tier specification goal to aim for depends on the business needs. The business must weigh its design goals against the investment implications.

A data center with applications running tasks that can be managed manually for a short period without any significant impact on revenue can make do with Tier I data center. To reduce the possible downtime period, the business can invest in redundancies to some components, like the UPS, or fully upscale to Tier II.

Most data center owners have found that aiming for a Tier III rating has an economically efficient reliability outcome when compared to Tier IV data centers, which are significantly more expensive to operate, as all the capacity components need to work concurrently.

Installing standard operational procedures and a rigorous maintenance regime in a Tier III data center can prevent unplanned outages of which Tier IV data centers are tolerant, at a lower cost.

However, for applications that are highly intolerant any sort of outage, investing in a Tier IV data center might make more economic sense as against the incurred revenue losses that the outage would cause.

We looked at a few topologies in the previous pages. Can you determine the possible Tier outcomes?

CHAPTER FIVE
ENERGY EFFICIENCY

The Need for Energy Efficiency

As more and more services get offered and consumed digitally, more and more IT equipment are deployed.

As more and more IT equipment are deployed, more and more data centers are commissioned.

As more and more data centers are commissioned, more and more power is needed.

As more and more power is needed, more and more electrical energy is generated and used.

As more and more electrical energy is used, there is more and more reason for us to worry as a race. We are continuously altering our ecological landscape. The fact that data centers have to run 24 x 365 hours in a year certainly does not help.

The worry stems from the *how* through which electrical energy is generated, and the *what* that happens to the electrical energy after is used.

Energy cannot be created or destroyed, only transformed. Electrical energy is generated through the transformation from other sources. And after usage by IT equipment, it is transformed into another form.

The most common energy form from which electrical energy is generated is through chemical energy stored in fossil fuels. The actual mechanism is out of our scope, but it suffices to say that the fuels are burned. The burning releases energy in the form of heat before other eventual transformations to electricity.

Some of the heat generated is lost to the environment. In addition, some gases are emitted to the atmosphere, most of which are bad for the environment, especially the carbon brothers, Carbon Dioxide (CO_2) and Carbon Monoxide (CO). CO eventually becomes CO_2 anyway, after exposure to Oxygen in the atmosphere.

When the IT equipment use power, the electrical energy consumed is transformed to heat energy. Which is also emitted to the environment.

The heat energies for generation and usage, coupled with the release of so-called greenhouse gases (chiefly CO_2) to the earth's atmosphere, have the collective effect of changing the earth's natural atmospheric circumstances, a phenomenon known as Global Warming[3]. There is ample literature on the likely effects of global warming. In summary, it is **not** good.

This grim reality will certainly not shut down data centers. It behooves us, data center designers, to find

---

[3] Climate Change, also called Global Warming, refers to the rise in average surface temperatures on Earth.

creative and efficient ways of generating, and minimizing, usage of energy in our data centers.

The Data Center is not the only building that uses energy, some would argue. Why must it the prerogative of designers to prioritize energy efficiency? Well, for starters, a typical enterprise data center may consume as much as 40 times as much energy a similarly sized office would consume.

Beyond altruism, worrying about energy efficiency has a significant impact on the bottom-line. Energy costs continue to rise, especially against the backdrop of the unstable political landscape. Industry regulators have also started to apply pressure to enforce environmental restrictions.

Data Center Power System designers need to explore ways to reduce dependence on carbon-based energy sources. Renewable energy technologies are becoming a lot more mature and mainstream. It is time for them to take a prominent role in the data center.

Industry surveys carried out around 2017 revealed that data centers account for up to 3% of global electricity usage. That number is closer to 5% today, and these numbers will keep increasing.

The data center stakeholders must place energy efficiency front, back, and center. And that starts with saving as much energy as possible.

Energy Efficiency Metrics

It is common knowledge in management circles that if you want real growth and results, you need to measure what matters. *What matters* are the indicators, key metrics that show whether you are achieving your objectives, and if not, how far off the objectives you are.

Our objective is to ensure as much energy efficiency as possible. We want to make sure we generate only as much as we need. And we want as much as possible to minimize what we need.

When we generate, we don't want to lose potential electrical energy to other forms of energy. We want to convert almost, if not all, the energy from our source to electrical energy.

How do we know if we are achieving our objectives or not? Whether to pat ourselves at the back or return to the drawing board? Whether to double down on what we are doing or step backward? We know through energy efficiency indicators.

The data center industry has agreed upon some metrics to measure data center energy performance. The most well-known of this is the Power Usage Effectives, or PUE for short.

Power Usage Effectiveness

Power usage effectiveness (PUE) is a value that shows how much of the power being generated by the facility is actually used by the IT equipment for which it is generated.

Originally published in 2007 by The Green Grid, a consortium of participants from different facets of the data center ecosystem dedicated to improving data center efficiency, the PUE has become a global standard, published in 2016 under ISO/IEC 30134-2:2016.

PUE helps measure the objective of wanting to make sure we generate only as much energy as we need.

The only reason the data center exists is to house the IT equipment that support the business' IT strategy. It would make sense that the bulk of the energy generated is used to power these IT equipment. Data center designers need to find creative ways to reduce the amount of energy needed to power other supporting equipment, like cooling, security, monitoring, lighting, etc. We will discuss design efficiency options for different systems in future publications.

The PUE is calculated as follows:

$$PUE = \frac{Total\ available\ energy\ in\ the\ facilty}{Total\ energy\ used\ by\ IT\ equipment}$$

Or

$$PUE = 1 + \frac{Total\ energy\ used\ by\ non\text{-}IT\ equipment}{Total\ energy\ used\ by\ IT\ equipment}$$

Notice that the formula says *Energy* instead of *Power*. Recall from Physics that:

$$Energy\ (kWh) = Power\ (kW) \times Time\ (h)$$

The PUE for a data center is usually computed annually. However, given the nature of the formula, the PUE will have the same value if we simply use the power consumption at a given point in time (kW) or the power consumption over a period of time (kWh).[4] Nevertheless, for the avoidance of doubt, the PUE is an energy metric.

For example, assume a data center generates as much as 10,000 kW of power. Of this, 3,000kW is used to power the servers. Another 1,000kW is used by the switches, routers, and other network equipment. The gigantic storage array uses just 2,000kW.

The operators use 1000kW for their PCs, and other monitoring and security infrastructure in the Network Operating Center (NOC). They use another 500kW in their living quarters.

The entire cooling plant requires 2,000kW to function. And the remaining 500kW is used to light the entire facility.

---

[4] The power value ought to be multiplied by the number of hours under consideration. However, since both the numerator and denominator are measured over the same period, their time values cancel each other out.

From the above scenario, how is the PUE computed? Try to calculate it before flipping over to the next page. Remember that the PUE is to help us measure the objective of wanting to make sure we generate only as much energy as we need.

$$PUE = \frac{10000 \; kW}{3000 \; kW + 1000 \; kW + 2000 \; kW} = 1.67$$

Or

$$PUE = 1 + \frac{1000 \; kW + 500 \; kW + 2000 \; kW + 500 \; kW}{3000 \; kW + 1000 \; kW + 2000 \; kW}$$
$$= 1.67$$

According to this metric, a data center is at its most efficient when the PUE value equals 1.0. The farther away from 1.0 this value is, the more inefficient the data center. The data center in our scenario can be said to be reasonably efficient. The Uptime Institute, a standards body that certifies data center compliance to the tiers[5], estimates that most data centers have an average PUE of 2.5.

---

[5] Data Center Tiers is a system used to describe data center infrastructure. Tiers will be discussed later in this book.

The best thing about the PUE is that it gives designers and operators a target to aim at. Improvements can continuously be made on equipment, layout, topologies, etc, throughout the life cycle of the data center.

As at the publication of this book, the most efficient data center in the world, in the light of PUE, is the Facebook data center in Luleå, Sweden. This data center has a PUE of just 1.1. The Apple data center in North Carolina, USA, is also said to also have a PUE of 1.1. However, Apple has not made this data public.

Data Center Infrastructure Efficiency

Data Center Infrastructure Efficiency (DCiE) is another data center efficiency metric. As the name implies, it is a value, expressed in percentage, that specifies how efficient a data center is. A value of 100% indicates the highest possible efficiency.

Also developed by the Green Grid, DCiE is the inverse of PUE expressed in percentage. DCiE is calculated as follows:

$$DCiE = \frac{Total\ energy\ used\ by\ IT\ equipment}{Total\ energy\ power\ in\ the\ facility} \times 100\%$$

Or

$$DCiE = \frac{1}{PUE} \times 100\%$$

Returning to our previous example, the DCiE for the data center is computed thus:

$$DCiE = \frac{3000 \text{ kW} + 1000 \text{ kW} + 2000 \text{ kW}}{10000 \text{ kW}} \times 100\%$$

$$= 60\%$$

Or

$$DCiE = \frac{1}{1.67} \times 100\% = 60\%$$

The Data Center can be said to be moderately efficient.

DCiE helps put the PUE figures in a better perspective. The Facebook and Amazon data centers sited above have a DCiE of 90%.

Data Center designers and operators should aim for an average DCiE value of 70%, or a PUE value of 1.4. This will help save real costs, in the margins of the investors, and the longevity of our planet.

Compute Power Efficiency

In 2007, another metric, Compute Power Efficiency (CPE)[6], came on the horizon. The PUE and DCiE assume that power delivered to IT equipment is being used to perform useful work for the business. But this is not the case in all cases. Sometimes, IT equipment consume power without doing anything. This power is a wastage not factored in the PUE and DCiE metrics. The CPE attempts to remedy that.

The CPE attempts to measure the actual efficiency of the data center while considering the fact that some of the power being transferred to IT equipment is not actually transformed for use, but is instead lost to heat.

CPE is calculated similarly to DCiE, but it takes into account the actual utilization of the IT equipment. The formula for CPE is as follows:

$$CPE = \frac{\%\ IT\ Equipment\ Utilization \times Total\ IT\ Energy}{Total\ Facility\ Energy}$$

Or

$$CPE = \frac{\%\ IT\ Equipment\ Utilization}{PUE}$$

---

[6] This metric was proposed in their paper in the paper "Metrics and an Infrastructure Model to Evaluate Data Center Efficiency" (Belady and Malone, 2007)

Assume the data center in our example has an IT equipment utilization of 80%. That means IT equipment collectively remain idle 20% of the time, while still consuming the same amount of power. Calculating the CPE, we have:

$$CPE = \frac{80\% \times 6000\ kW}{10000\ kW} = 48\%$$

As you can see, instead of a respectable score of 60%, we get an efficiency value of 48%. That is below average.

While recognizing the validity of its premise, the CPE as a metric however presents a notable challenge. How do we measure IT equipment utilization? For servers, using the CPU work rate may be the obvious choice, but other server components also perform work. There may IO intensive operations while the CPU remains idle. Modern workloads are now being designed to work entirely in memory. What about Storage, and Network, how do we measure utilization?

These difficulties led the Green Grid to develop another efficiency metric, Data Center Energy Productivity (DCeP).

Data Center Energy Productivity

The Data Center Energy Productivity (DCeP) metric aims to measure the *useful work* produced by the data center given the amount of energy it consumes. Rather than simply focusing on IT equipment utilization like the CPE, DCeP is more holistic in that it concedes that useful work can be done even when the IT equipment is seemingly idle. DCeP is expressed as follows:

$$DCeP = \frac{Useful\ Work\ Produced}{Total\ Energy\ Consumed\ Producing\ this\ Work}$$

There is a reason why PUE is still the most common metric for measuring data center efficiency - its simplicity. Despite a sound theoretical basis, DCeP is still not widely utilized in the industry. It is too complicated. It took five years for the Green Grid to unveil this metric after initial work began in 2008. You will see why in a moment.

Recall again from Physics that:

$$Energy\ (J) = Power\ (W) \times Time\ (s)$$

As the ERE is an energy metric, computation will require measuring the power consumed over a given period of time, what the Green Grid terms as the *assessment period*.

Again, how do you determine useful work? The Green Grid makes clear that useful work is implied in the unique context of the data center in question. It is expressed by the equation:

$$Useful\ Work = \sum_{i=1}^{N} V_i \times U_i(t,T) \times T_i$$

Where

N = total number of tasks initiated during the assessment window

V_i = normalization factor that allows the tasks to be summed numerically

T_i = 1, if task i completes during the assessment window; 0, if task i does not complete during the window

$U_i(t,T)$ = time-based utility function for each task i, where the parameter t is elapsed time from initiation to completion of the task, and T is the absolute time of completion of the task.

As you can see from the above, calculating the DCeP requires the manual computation of the normalization factor and utility function of each and every type of task that takes place in the data center. The operator would then:

- determine an assessment window,
- document all the tasks that took place during the assessment window,
- calculate the total energy consumed during the assessment window,
- applying the appropriate normalization factor and utility function on each task to make it numerically summable
- adding together the normalized values for each task to determine the useful work
- dividing the useful work by the measured consumed energy to determine the DCeP

The assessment time should be at least 20 times the average runtime of any of the tasks to be started.

A theoretical framework on how to determine the normalization factors and utility functions is best left to the realms of academia. You could also work out these values alongside other stakeholders in your data center.

Energy Reuse Effectiveness

We know that data center discharges used energy in the form of heat, mostly from the servers. From the Law of

Conservation of Energy, we know that the energy from this heat is still useful. It can be collected and channeled, or transformed, for other uses, in the data center or other adjacent buildings, therefore reducing the aggregate energy generated and heat lost to the atmosphere.

Energy Reuse Effectiveness (ERE), also developed the Green Grid, was developed to recognize this possibility. A data center can have a high PUE, but still be efficient by channeling the lost energy to heat buildings, work areas, domestic waters, or other useful causes.

Like DCeP, ERE also requires an assessment period. Assuming the assessment period is annual, ERE is calculated as follows:

$$ERE = \frac{Energy\ used\ by\ Facility - Energy\ reused}{Energy\ used\ by\ IT\ Equipment}$$

Where,

Facility Energy, IT Energy, and Energy Reuse are estimated over the course of one full year

Returning to our previous example where total power used by the facility was 10,000kW and IT equipment only used 6,000kW out of this. Assuming 3,000kW of generated power is being reused,

$$ERE = \frac{(10000 \text{ kW} \times 1 \text{ year}) - (3000 \text{ kW} \times 1 \text{ year})}{(6000 \text{ kW} \times 1 \text{ year})}$$

$$= 1.17$$

which is more respected efficiency value than 1.67.

A derivative of the ERE is the Energy Reuse Factor (ERF), which is the ratio of reused energy to total facility energy.

$$ERF = \frac{Energy\ reused}{Energy\ used\ by\ Facility}$$

Or

$$ERF = 1 - \frac{ERE}{PUE}$$

Calculating the ERF of our reference data center,

$$ERF = \frac{3000 \text{ kW} \times 1 \text{ year}}{10000 \text{ kW} \times 1 \text{ year}} = 0.3$$

Or

$$ERF = 1 - \frac{1.17}{1.67} = 0.3$$

Conversely, the ERE can be computed from the PUE when the ERF is known.

$$ERE = PUE \times (1 - ERF)$$
$$= 1.67 \times (1 - 0.3)$$
$$= 1.17$$

Carbon Usage Effectiveness

As mentioned previously CO_2, is a major contributor to the problem of global warming. The Carbon Usage Effectiveness (CUE) aims to address this problem by help data center stakeholders control their CO_2 emissions. CUE is a sustainability metric, and is calculated as follows:

$$CUE = \frac{Total\ CO2\ emissions\ caused\ by\ Total\ Facility\ Energy}{Total\ IT\ Equipment\ Energy}$$

Unlike PUE which is unit-less and has an ideal value of 1.0, CUE has dimensions ($kgCO_2eq/kWh$) and has an ideal value of 0.0. The objective of the data center stakeholders should be to reduce their CUE values as much as possible.

The CUE is a source-based metric, rather than a site-based metric. Therefore, it considers CO_2 emissions directly as a result of energy being generated for use by the data center. Energy to the data center facility can come from the government-generated utility or local generating capacity. Therefore, for the sake of completion, the formula can be re-written as follows:

$$CUE = \frac{Total\ CO2\ emissions\ caused\ by\ Grid\text{-}Sourced\ Energy + Total\ CO2\ emissions\ caused\ by\ onsite\ Energy}{Total\ IT\ Equipment\ Energy}$$

CO_2 emissions from onsite generators can be measured in real-time using CO_2 meters or calculated from generator manufacturer specifications. CO_2 emissions due to grid-sourced energy can be read from government or international agency published data. Where this is inadequate, and the PUE is known, we can compute the CUE from the Carbon Emission Factor (CEF) as follows:

$$CUE = [(\%E_g \times CEF_g) + (\%E_s \times CEF_s)] \times PUE$$

ENERGY EFFICIENCY

Where

%E_g is percentage of facility energy sourced from the grid,

CEF_g is the CO_2 emitted per unit energy from grid source measured in $kgCO_2eq/kWh$,

%E_s is percentage of facility energy sourced from the onsite generators,

CEF_s is the CO_2 emitted per unit energy from onsite generators measured in $kgCO_2eq/kWh$

The CEF value from grid sources can be acquired from government published data for the region where the site is based, over the course of the time period under consideration. The CEF value from onsite generators can be acquired from manufacturer published documentations, or calculated manually using the formula:

$$CEF = \frac{CO2\ emitted\ from\ onsite\ generators\ (kgCO2eq)}{Total\ energy\ from\ onsite\ generators\ (kWh)}$$

The above are just a few metrics used to gauge the efficiency of data centers relative to generated energy. Other metrics exist to measure other aspects, like cooling.

These metrics do not exist to compare data centers. Indeed, data centers located in hot regions cannot possibly take advantage of free cooling technologies available to data centers in more brumal areas, consequently driving PUE measures up. The metrics, when taken together, are meant to help data center designers, operators, and other stakeholders, creatively bring about the most efficient data center they possibly can, considering their peculiar circumstances.

Energy Efficiency Certification Standards

Data centers can lay claim to being energy-efficient, and support those claims by bandying figures about. However, how can potential clients, partners, and the industry at large verify those claims? This is where standards and certification bodies come into play. The most widely accepted standard for rating a building's energy efficiency is Leadership in Energy and Environmental Design (LEED).

LEED

The U.S. Green Building Council (USGBC), developed a standard for rating buildings based on energy efficiency. This standard is known as LEED (Leadership in Energy and Environmental Design).

LEED provides a framework for designing, building, and operating structures to improve performance on environmental sustainability. It measures efficiency on water usage, energy usage, CO_2 emission savings, resource management, and other metrics that matter in addressing the threat of Climate Change.

Data centers can achieve a Certified, Silver, Gold, or Platinum certification depending on their accrued ratings. The specific LEED certification to pursue will depend on the building type and building phase. For data centers to be newly constructed or renovated, the applicable LEED is **BD+C** (Building Design and Construction). For existing data centers with little or no construction work, the LEED to pursue is **O+M** (Building Operations and Maintenance).

You can learn more about LEED from the U.S. Green Building Council website here: **https://www.usgbc.org/help/what-leed**

BREEAM

BREEAM stands for Building Research Establishment Assessment Method. BREEAM is a certification program that validates a building's compliance with environmental, social, and economic sustainability performance standards specified by the Building Research Establishment (BRE).

The BRE is an organization headquartered in the UK that engages in research, consultancy, training, and standards development. Originally a government establishment set up as far back as 1921, the BRE was fully privatized in 1997.

While BREEAM was first launched in 1990, data center specific standards were only introduced in 2010.

Following an assessment, buildings are issued a BREEAM certificate with one to six stars. One star indicates an Acceptable rating, two stars a Pass rating, three stars a Good rating, four stars a Very Good rating, five stars an Excellent rating, and six stars an Outstanding rating.

Further information on the BREEAM certification can be found on the BREEAM website here: **https://www.breeam.com/discover/how-breeam-certification-works/.**

ENERGY STAR

The Energy Star program was started in 1992 as part of the U.S. Federal Clean Air Act. The program is run by the U.S Environmental Protection Agency (EPA) alongside the US Department of Energy (DOE). The program helps individuals, homes, and commercial buildings save costs due to energy usage, and at the same time, protect the environment from exposure to greenhouse gases.

ENERGY EFFICIENCY

The Energy Star program covers three main aspects - Products, Homes, and Commercial Businesses. Compliance with the relevant program guidelines earns such Product, Home, or Commercial Business an ENERGY STAR® label. You have probably seen some products with the ENERGY STAR® label clearly displayed. A complete list of products with the Energy Star label® is maintained on the Energy Star website here: **https://www.energystar.gov/products.**

While products with an ENERGY STAR® rating might cost more to acquire than their non-efficient counterparts, the difference is eventually recouped in savings from energy costs, with the additional bonus of a sustainable environment.

Products are certified under the **ENERGY STAR Products program**, homes are covered under the **Home Performance with ENERGY STAR program**, while commercial businesses are rated under the **Commercial Building Energy Asset Score program.** Data Centers will fall under the Commercial Businesses category.

Energy Star certification is given to buildings with a high Energy Star score[7]. The score is a unit-less figure between 1 and 100. Data center stakeholders should work at getting a score as close as possible to 100, by

---

[7] Information on how the Energy Star score is calculated is available on the Energy Star website: https://www.energystar.gov/buildings/tools-and-resources/portfolio-manager-technical-reference-energy-star-score

adopting energy-efficient practices and using IT equipment with the ENERGY STAR® rating.

Energy Efficiency Best Practices

There are several opportunities to optimize energy use in the data center. Some of these include:

Virtualization

Virtualization is the practice of consolidating several IT workloads into a single piece of physical hardware. The consolidated workloads exist as 'virtual' systems and are visible to the network as if they are separate independent hardware.

Virtualization practice started with servers. A virtual server is a software implementation that runs programs like a real physical server. A single piece of physical hardware can have several virtual servers running on it.

IT practices typically dedicate a server for every software service offered. Prior to virtualization, that meant a separate server for every new service. Now, with virtualization, a single piece of hardware can be used to run several services.

Over time, virtualization technology was developed to include network virtualization and storage virtualization. Current advances in technology have introduced the concept of the Software-Defined Data Center (SDDC) where every component of the data center is virtualized.

This has the net effect of reducing the physical footprint of IT equipment, thus saving energy.

Decommissioning Unused Equipment

Surveys in data centers have continuously found that several unused or underutilized IT equipment continue to run in data centers. This is because once a piece of equipment is set up in the data center, IT departments commence an operation regime that will keep the equipment running. Unfortunately, there are very few recurring audits to affirm the usefulness or utilization of these idling capacities. Monitoring approaches typically only watch for uptime or overutilization.

In addition to accrued energy savings, consolidating workloads and then decommissioning the freed-up servers has a significant potential for savings in operation costs such as licensing and maintenance. The unused equipment can be sold off for additional revenue.

Storage Management

Data storage accounts for the fastest-growing need for equipment in the data center. As more daily operations are migrated to the digital domain, data generation continues to accelerate. The generated data needs to be stored and retained for long periods.

Several advances in storage technology have made it possible to store much more data with less hardware. Some of these technologies include Data Deduplication, Data Compression, Thin Provisioning, Snapshots, Tiered Storage, Automated Storage Provisioning, Solid State Drives, etc.

It is important that IT departments utilize efficient storage mechanisms and lower the energy for storage needs.

Energy-efficient Equipment

We have discussed the ENERGY STAR Products program. IT and data center operators should endeavor to utilize energy-efficient equipment in the data center.

A list of energy-efficient data center equipment are maintained on the ENERGY STAR website here: **https://www.energystar.gov/products/data_center_equipment/**

The above has been a discussion on cooling efficiency for the data center. Data center designers should endeavor to work with cooling experts to design highly energy-efficient data centers.

Next we will examine the codes and standards relevant to cooling in the data center.

CHAPTER SIX
CODES AND STANDARDS

To maintain a minimum standard for quality and safety, every country has supervisory bodies that set regulations, rules and codes defining electrical installations. Flouting these rules may have legal implications. Hence, the data center power systems designer needs to be familiar with the applicable rules set by the Authorities Having Jurisdiction (AHJ) in their region.

In addition to the local AHJs, there are globally recognized bodies that set standards for data center design. These standards exist to streamline design practices so that all data centers complying with the standards can provide the same outcome, regardless of geographical location.

Some of the well-known standards bodies include the following:

Uptime Institute

The very first and most widely recognized standards body is the Uptime Institute, which came up with the Tier rating system in 1995. They meticulously define that the Tier rating system measures data center design outcomes, differing greatly from other standards, which detail specific checklists that must be followed.

Data Center designs are classified as either Tier I, Tier II, Tier III, or Tier IV, depending on design objectives and outcomes. The highest tier level does not necessarily indicate the best design, rather it is business objectives that determine the best tier level to target.

Details of the Uptime Institute Tier Classification can be seen here:

https://uptimeinstitute.com/tiers

TIA

The Telecommunications Industry Association (TIA) is a body renowned for network cabling standards. Its cabling standards cover Buildings, Campuses, and more recently, Data Centers.

The TIA, in conjunction with the American National Standards Institute (ANSI), created the TIA-942 Data Center Standard in 2005. A revision was issued in 2010, named TIA-942-B.

Initially, the TIA 942 built on Uptime Institute's Tier Classification system, providing additional directives for network cabling topology, power, cooling, monitoring, security, building services, civil works, and many more. However, owing to disagreements over how the standards should be laid out (outcome-based or following a strict set of rules), Uptime Institute retrieved the right to publish their standards from TIA.

TIA-942-B revision is very specific and detailed on its tier rating and the attendant requirements for each level of redundancy and availability.

Details of the TIA 942 standard can be seen here:

https://global.ihs.com/doc_detail.cfm?&csf=TIA&document_name=TIA%2D942&item_s_key=00414811

BICSI

As at the time TIA was working on its Data Center Standard, the Building Industry Consulting Service International Inc. (BICSI) was also working on theirs. The BICSI issued its standard, BICSI 002-2010: Data Center Design and Implementation Best Practices, also in 2010.

In many respects, the BICSI 002-2010 is similar to TIA 942. Many of both passages can be mapped to each other. Only in minute details do both documents disagree.

Also, just as the TIA standard has undergone a revision, BICSI has also updated its standard with a new release: ANSI/BICSI 002-2019, Data Center Design and Implementation Best Practices.

The BICSI standard however does not specify a tier rating system. It only details best practices and recommendations as well as references to external organizations' standards, such as those from the American Society of Heating, Refrigerating, and Air-Conditioning Engineers (ASHRAE).

Details of the NSI/BICSI 002-2019 standard can be found here:

https://www.bicsi.org/standards/available-standards-store/single-purchase/ansi-bicsi-002-2019-data-center-design

ASHRAE

The American Society of Heating, Refrigerating and Air-Conditioning Engineers (ASHRAE) is a global society dedicated to advancing the arts and sciences of heating, ventilation, air conditioning, and refrigeration to serve humanity and promote a sustainable world. Founded in 1894, ASHRAE publishes journals, whitepapers, technical resources, and global standards that advance its objective, which is *"to serve humanity by advancing the arts and sciences of heating, ventilation, air conditioning, refrigeration, and their allied fields"*.

ASHRAE publishes and maintains a standard that establishes the minimum energy efficiency requirements for the design and operation of data centers, the ASHRAE 90.4 standard. The current iteration of the standard is the 2019 update, the ANSI/ASHRAE Standard 90.4-2019, Energy Standard for Data Centers.

Standard 90.4 offers a framework for the energy-efficient design of data centers with special consideration to their unique load requirements compared to other buildings. The standard was developed under the guiding principle that data centers are mission-critical facilities demanding careful attention to the potential impact of its requirements.

Details about the standard and requirements for compliance are available here:

https://www.techstreet.com/ashrae/standards/ashrae-90-4-2019?product_id=2092750

In addition to its data center standard, ASHRAE also has a standing technical committee, the ASHRAE TC10.1, which is concerned with the industrial applications of standard or special equipment to meet specific refrigeration requirements.

NFPA

The National Fire Protection Association (NFPA) is a global organization headquartered in the USA. It is set up with the goal of avoiding loss of, or injury to, life, property, or economic activity due to fire, electricity, or other related hazards.

CODES AND STANDARDS

To achieve this aim, the NFPA defines codes and standards which, when followed, will mitigate the risk of fire and electrical related incidences. The NFPA also releases publications and hold conferences to raise more awareness about its work.

The NFPA standard relevant to data center power systems is the NFPA 70 or National Electric Code (NEC®).

CENELEC

The Comité Européen de Normalisation Electrotechnique, or the European Committee for Electrotechnical Standardization is responsible for standardization in the electrotechnical engineering field in Europe.

CENELEC acts as a platform for experts to develop European Standards (ENs). The standards are based on a consensus, which reflects the economic and social interests of its member countries.

The CENELEC standard relevant to data center power systems is the EN 50110-1.

IET

The Institution of Engineering and Technology (IET) is a global professional engineering institution, with its main offices in the UK.

The IET publishes rules and regulations on multidisciplinary engineering fields, and is empowered by Law in the UK to issue professional registration for the titles of Chartered Engineer, Incorporated Engineer, Engineering Technician, and ICT Technician, in the UK.

The IET standard relevant to data center power systems is the BS 7671, which it co-publishes with the British Standards Institution (BSI).

BSI

The British Standards Institution (BSI) is the body responsible for national standards in the UK. The BSI-issued standards cover a wide range of fields, products, and services.

In addition to its own standards, the BSI assesses other European and international standards, and modifies as it sees fit. It also adopts other standards that are in tandem with its own[8]

---

[8] Standards adopted from CENELEC are prefixed BS EN, from ISO are prefixed BS ISO, and so on.

CODES AND STANDARDS

The BSI standard relevant to data center power systems is the BS 7671, which it co-publishes with the Institution of Engineering and Technology (IET).

IEC

The International Electrotechnical Commission (IEC) is the leading global body responsible for the preparation and publication of International Standards for all electrical, electronic, and related technologies, collectively known as *electrotechnology*.

Along with its sister organizations, the International Organization for Standardization (ISO) and the International Telecommunication Union (ITU), the IEC develops international standards applicable worldwide and ensures that international standards complement and fit well with each other. The IEC standards relevant to data center power systems are IEC 60364 and IEC 61936.

The objectives of all the standards are the same. A lot of work has been done, and is continuously being done, to bring all the different standards as close together as possible.

The data center designer must understand the relevant standards and local regulations to ensure safety and avoid problems with the Law.

While some of the standards only provide industry recommendations and best practices, some provisions of some of the standards are statutory. European standards are usually followed in Europe while the US-based facilities follow US standards. Other parts of the world follow either European or US standards or both.

The data center designer should be familiar with relevant regulatory and industry standards and guidelines appropriate to his/her region to design a data center that achieves the expected business outcomes.

CHAPTER SEVEN

TEN -STEP FRAMEWORK

In the previous chapters, we outlined and discussed the various aspects to consider when designing the power system for the data center. You should now be sufficiently equipped to be a valuable member of a data center power design team.

Now, take a moment to structure out your design process if tasked with a data center project, given all the information you now possess.

Or, simply use my Ten-Step Framework.

The Ten-Step framework is a simple, repeatable process consisting of ten steps. Each step accomplishes a task that has been discussed in this book. The input to the process is information about the business' needs, while the output is a design diagram and the Bill of Materials (BOM) which, when deployed, will accomplish the business goal.

The Ten Steps

The ten steps are described below:

1) Tier

Determine the data center tier level as dictated by the business need. Speak with the relevant stakeholders involved in decision making. Understand why the business needs a data center, the problems it needs to solve, the outcomes it expects to realize, and the budget it is willing to spend. Takedown the expected power the IT loads to be deployed will consume and the downtimes it can tolerate.

Select the tier level to design based on information from these conversations.

2) Space

After determining the tier level, look at the space which is proposed to house the data center. Remember, it is not only racks that will be in the data center. We will possibly need to position transformers, engine generators, UPS, batteries, switchgear (high, medium, and low voltage), transfer switches, and any other path elements. We will also need a path to route cables through.

Work with an architect, draughtsman, or other specialists to highlight any space and environmental constraints.

3) Need

With the information from the Tier step above, determine the need (N) of the data center. Work out the required sizes of the capacity components.

4) Components

Armed with the capacity requirements and space constraints, seek out the capacity components you will use. Work with the relationships you already have with vendors, colleagues, manufacturers, etc. Perform copious research on affordable technologies available.

Select energy-efficient capacity components that will deliver the required capacity after applying environmental constraints. If you need to combine two or more components to get N, determine any required component or any factor that, if not used, might inadvertently diminish the combined capacity.

5) Schematic

Draw out the electrical schematic or block diagram. Decide on the elements and the path through which power will get to the IT equipment. Include all redundancies demanded by the tier level in capacity components and path elements.

6) Optimize

Take a second look at the drawn schematic. Every component on the diagram is an additional cost, in terms of initial capital outlay, and in terms of continuous operation. We want our design to be efficient, and deliver the outcomes at minimal cost. Can you tweak the design to allow for the removal of any component or element? Ensure that any removal will not defeat the planned tier level.

7) Earthing

After finalizing the capacity components and the path elements that will drive the required outcomes, draw out the schematic for equipotential bonding.

Work with an electrical technician to link to any existing grounding in the facility.

8) Sizing

Based on the final approved schematics, calculate the required sizes of cables, circuit breakers, transfer switches, and any other path element depending on the amount of current that will flow through the path element.

TEN-STEP FRAMEWORK

9) Positioning

Work with the architect or draughtsman to layout the capacity components and path elements in the earmarked spaces. Following the marked cable routes, measure the required lengths of each and every wire and cable.

10) BOM

List out all the contents of the electrical and bonding schematics. Include the quantities and measured lengths. Submit this and the schematics to your boss.

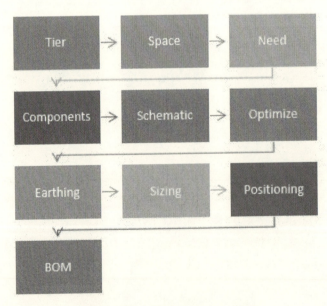

The Ten-Step Framework

Case Study

A company recently invented a revolutionary technology and intend to offer it as a service over the Internet. The company commits to its prospective clients in its service agreements that the service will be available 99.9% of the time. Flouting the service agreements can have legal and financial implications.

For starters, the company wants to set up 60 racks, each containing IT equipment that consume an average of 4kW. If the business goes well, the company will scale up the racks to 100.

Design the power system for this data center using the Ten-Step Framework. Assume there are no space or environmental constraints.

You can share your design with me by email at dcbadru@gmail.com. I will be happy to provide feedback. I am also running a course on the Ten-Step Framework where I will hold your hand as you go through step-by-step. Fire me an email if you want to be part of the next cohort.

NEXT STEPS

The foregoing has been a detailed discussion on designing Power for the Data Center.

You may find this sufficient for your needs, or you may decide to probe further. You will find that there are other aspects of the Data Center in need of your design prowess. You may be interested in designing Cooling, Communications, Safety, Security, Spaces, Monitoring, and Management for the Data Center.

Other books are set to be published to specifically address the design of all the different aspects of the data center.

Join the waiting list, http://eepurl.com/g-ZkNr, to get notified as soon as they are released.

You may need some help on a particular project you are working on, or you might just wish to provide some feedback.

Either way, you can send me an email at dcbadru@gmail.com for your Data Center inquiries.

To your success!

B.A. Ayomaya

BIBLIOGRAPHY

Anthony C. Fischer-Cripps (2004). *The electronics companion.* CRC Press. ISBN 978-0-7503-1012-3.

Authoritative Dictionary of Standards Terms (7th ed.), IEEE, 2000, ISBN 978-0-7381-2601-2, Std. 100

Avoiding Trap Doors Associated with Purchasing a UPS System" (PDF). Archived from the original (PDF) on 2013-03-26. Retrieved 2018-12-11.

Bagotskii, Vladimir Sergeevich (2006). *Fundamentals of electrochemistry.* ISBN 978-0-471-70058-6.

Bolioli, T.; Duggirala, M.; Haines, E.; Kolappan, R.; Wong, H. (2009), *Version 5.0 System Implementation* (PDF) (white paper), Energy Star

Boylestad, Robert (2002). *Introductory Circuit Analysis (10th ed.).* ISBN 978-0-13-097417-4.

Brown, Forbes T. (2006). *Engineering System Dynamics*: A Unified Graph-Centered Approach(2nd ed.). Boca Raton, Florida: CRC Press. ISBN 978-0-8493-9648-9.

C. J. Brockman (1928) *The origin of voltaic electricity: The contact vs. chemical theory before the concept of E. M. F. was developed*, Journal of Chemical Education, vol. 5, no. 5.

Consoliver, Earl L.; Mitchell, Grover I. (1920). *Automotive ignition systems.* McGraw-Hill.

BIBLIOGRAPHY

Cotton, Bart (January 2005). *Battery Asset Management: VRLA ageing characteristics* (PDF). Batteries International. Archived from the original (PDF) on 2013-04-06.

Cottuli, Carol (2011), *Comparison of Static and Rotary UPS* (PDF), Schneider Electric, White Paper 92 rev. 2, retrieved April 7, 2012

Croft, Terrell; Summers, Wilford I. (1987). *American Electricians' Handbook (Eleventh ed.)*. New York: McGraw Hill. ISBN 0-07-013932-6.

Cutnell, John D.; Johnson, Kenneth W. (1992). *Physics (2nd ed.)*. New York: Wiley. ISBN 978-0-471-52919-4.

Demetrius T. Paris and F. Kenneth Hurd (1969), *Basic Electromagnetic Theory*. McGraw-Hill, New York, ISBN 0-07-048470-8

Ewald Fuchs; Mohammad A. S. Masoum (14 July 2015). *Power Quality in Power Systems and Electrical Machines*. Elsevier Science. ISBN 978-0-12-800988-8.

Fink, Donald G.; Beaty, H. Wayne (1978), *Standard Handbook for Electrical Engineers (11 ed.)*, New York: McGraw-Hill, ISBN 978-0-07-020974-9

Fluke 1760 Three-Phase Power Quality Recorder (PDF). Fluke Corporation. Retrieved 6 November 2017.

Generex. *Multi-XS User Manual* (PDF). Archived from the original (PDF) on 2012-01-27. Retrieved 2011-11-14.

Geng, Hwaiyu (2015). *Data Center Handbook*. Palo Alto, CA: John Wiley & Sons, Inc.

Hayt, William (1989). *Engineering Electromagnetics* (5th ed.). McGraw-Hill. ISBN 0070274061.

High-Availability Power Systems, Part I: UPS Internal Topology (PDF). Emerson Network power White Paper, 2000. Archived from the original (PDF) on 2013-03-26. Retrieved 2018-12-11.

High-Availability Power Systems, Part II: Redundancy Options (PDF). Emerson Network power White Paper, 2000. Archived from the original (PDF) on 2013-03-26. Retrieved 2018-12-11.

Horowitz, Paul; Hill, Winfield (2015). *The art of electronics (3rd ed.)*. Cambridge University Press. ISBN 978-0-521-80926-9.

How to calculate battery run-time. PowerStream Technologies. Retrieved 2010-04-26.

Howard M. Berlin, Frank C. Getz (1988), *Principles of Electronic Instrumentation and Measurement*, Merrill Pub. Co., 1988 ISBN 0-675-20449-6.

Ignacio J. Pérez-Arriaga (2014), *Regulation of the Power Sector*, Springer Science & Business Media ISBN 1447150341

International Bureau of Weights and Measures (2019-05-20), *SI Brochure: The International System of Units (SI) (PDF) (9th ed.)*, ISBN 978-92-822-2272-0

BIBLIOGRAPHY

Jaffe, Robert L.; Taylor, Washington (2018). *The physics of energy*. Cambridge University Press.

K. S. Suresh Kumar (2013), *Electric Circuit Analysis*, Pearson Education India, ISBN 9332514100

Kaiser, Kenneth L. (2004). *Electromagnetic Compatibility Handbook*. Boca Raton, Florida: CRC Press. ISBN 978-0-8493-2087-3.

Leonardo Energy. *Maintenance Manager's Guide, Section 2.1*. Retrieved August 1, 2012.

McDonald, John D. (2016). *Electric Power Substations Engineering (2nd ed.)*. Boca Raton, Florida: CRC Press. ISBN 978-1-4200-0731-2.

Michael F. Hordeski (2005). *Emergency and backup power sources: preparing for blackouts and brownouts*. The Fairmont Press, Inc. ISBN 9780881734850.

Oliver Heaviside (1894). *Electrical papers*. *1*. Macmillan and Co. ISBN 978-0-8218-2840-3.

Open Compute Project. Available at http://www.opencompute.org/.

P. Hammond (1969), *Electromagnetism for Engineers*. Pergamon Press, OCLC 854336.

Peter M. Curtis (2011). *Maintaining Mission Critical Systems in a 24/7 Environment*. Wiley. ISBN 9781118041628.

Power Factor Correction (PFC) Basics (PDF) (application note), Fairchild Semiconductor, 2004, archived from the original (PDF) on 2014-06-11, retrieved 2009-11-29

Program Requirements for Computers (PDF) (Version 5.0 ed.), US: Energy Star

R. Feynman; et al. *The Feynman Lectures on Physics.* Vol. II Ch. 22: AC Circuits. Caltech. Retrieved 4 December 2018.

Rasmussen, Neil (2011), *The Different Types of UPS Systems* (PDF), Schneider Electric, White Paper 1 rev. 7, retrieved April 7, 2012

Raymond, Eric Steven. *UPS HOWTO*, section 3.3. The Linux Documentation Project, 2003–2007.

Robert A. Millikan and E. S. Bishop (1917). *Elements of Electricity*. American Technical Society.

Robert N. Varney, Leon H. Fisher (1980), *Electromotive force: Volta's forgotten concept*, American Journal of Physics, vol. 48, iss. 5.

Rudolf Holze (2009), *Experimental Electrochemistry: A Laboratory Textbook*, John Wiley & Sons, ISBN 3527310983.

Sankaran, C. (1999), *Effects of Harmonics on Power Systems*, EC&M. Retrieved on 3 July 2012 from https://www.ecmweb.com/power-quality-reliability/article/20897053/effects-of-harmonics-on-power-systems

Saslow, Wayne M. (2002). *Electricity, Magnetism, and Light*. Toronto: Thomson Learning. pp. 302–4. ISBN 0-12-619455-6.

Sawyer R. (2011) *Calculating Total Power Requirements for Data Centers* (PDF), Schneider Electric, White Paper 3 rev. 1, retrieved April 7, 2018.

Schramm, Ben (2006), *Power Supply Design Principles: Techniques and Solutions, Part 3*, Newsletter, Nuvation, archived from the original on 2007-03-09

Scott Siddens (2007), *UPS on the front line*, Plant Engineering, archived from the original on 2009-11-09

Serway, Raymond A.; Jewett, John W. (2004). *Physics for Scientists and Engineers (6th ed.)*. Thomson Brooks/Cole. ISBN 0-534-40842-7.

Smith, Clare (2001). *Environmental Physics*. London: Routledge. ISBN 0-415-20191-8.

Solter, W. (2002), *A new international UPS classification by IEC 62040-3*, 24th Annual International Telecommunications Energy Conference, pp. 541–545, doi:10.1109/INTLEC.2002.1048709, ISBN 0-7803-7512-2, S2CID 195862090

Sugawara, I.; Suzuki, Y.; Takeuchi, A.; Teshima, T. (1997), *Experimental studies on active and passive PFC circuits*, INTELEC 97, 19th International Telecommunications Energy Conference, pp. 571–78, doi:10.1109/INTLEC.1997.646051, ISBN 978-0-7803-3996-5

T. L. Lowe, John Rounce (2002). *Calculations for A-level Physics*, Nelson Thornes, ISBN 0-7487-6748-7.

The International System of Units (SI) [SI brochure] (PDF). § 5.3.2 (p. 132, 40 in the PDF file): BIPM. 2006.

Ton, My; Fortenbery, Brian; Tschudi, William (January 2007). *DC Power for Improved Data Center Efficiency* (PDF). Lawrence Berkeley National Laboratory. Archived from the original (PDF) on 2010-10-08.

UPS Basics. Eaton Corporation. 2012. Retrieved 2014-01-08.

VanDee, Dawn (March 1, 1999), *"Rounding Up Rotary UPS Features"*, EC&M, Penton Business Media, retrieved April 7, 2012

Walker, Jearl; Halliday, David; Resnick, Robert (2014). *Fundamentals of physics (10th ed.)*. Hoboken, NJ: Wiley. ISBN 978-1118230732. OCLC 950235056.

Ward, M.R. (1971). *Electrical Engineering Science*. McGraw-Hill.

WT3000E Series Precision Power Analyzers (PDF). Yokogawa Corporation. Archived from the original (PDF) on 7 November 2017. Retrieved 6 November 2017.

Zangwill, Andrew (2013). *Modern Electrodynamics*. Cambridge University Press. ISBN 978-0-521-89697-9.

DESIGNING DATACENTERS
DATA CENTER DESIGN GUIDE
BOOK 1 - POWER

According to several surveys of data centers, power outage is the leading cause of data center downtimes.

Data Centers are a critical resource in the digital age. For many people, data center outages have tremendous impacts on day-to-day operations. For businesses, data center downtime can cause significant revenue losses.

This book is a detailed discussion on designing data center power systems. You will be introduced into the world of power, understand how it is generated, and learn how it is distributed. You will have a firm grasp of data center power needs, capacity requirements, power efficiency, and redundant topologies.

This is a must have book for every newbie data center designer. This is the book I wish I had when I started designing data center power systems. I trust you will feel the same way too. Experienced designers will also find it a helpful handbook.

About the Author

B.A. Ayomaya is a seasoned industry veteran and technology leader with a specific focus on the data center and digital systems. He has designed, architected, and implemented several data center and infrastructure initiatives in a career that has spanned almost two decades.

B.A. has had extensive experience managing technology teams, strategically developing and deploying systems and roadmaps that actualize business objectives.

DESIGNING DATACENTERS
DATA CENTER DESIGN GUIDE
BOOK 2 - COOLING

Specifying the requirements, Cooling Generation, Cooling Distribution, Cooling Efficiency, and Fault Tolerance for Data centers

B.A. AYOMAYA

DESIGNING DATACENTERS

Data Center Design Guide
BOOK 2: COOLING

Specifying the requirements, cooling generation, cooling distribution, cooling efficiency, and fault tolerance for data centers.

B.A. AYOMAYA

DISCLAIMER

All material used is original work or it has come from public domain sources e.g. the Internet. Should any copyright owner wish to have any items removed, then please contact the author at the following address: dcbadru@gmail.com.

Every effort has been made to provide accurate and complete information. However, the author assumes no responsibility for any direct, indirect, incidental, or consequential damages arising from the use of the information in this document.

Copyright © 2021 Badrudeen Ajibola Ayomaya.

All rights reserved.

No part of this publication may be reproduced, transmitted, transcribed, stored in a retrieval system, or translated into any language or computer language, in any form or by any means; electronic, mechanical, magnetic, chemical, thermal, manual, or otherwise, without the prior consent in writing of the copyright owner. Applications for the copyright owner's permission to reproduce any part of this publication should be sent to the copyright owner by email at the following address: **dcbadru@gmail.com**.

The book is sold subject to the condition that it shall not by way of trade, or otherwise, be lent, re-sold, hired out, or otherwise circulated without the copyright owner's prior consent in writing in any form of binding or cover other than in which it is published and without a similar condition including this condition being imposed on the subsequent purchaser.

Printed and published in the United States of America.

ISBN 9798705964529

"It is not the critic who counts; not the man who points out how the strong man stumbles, or where the doer of deeds could have done them better. The credit belongs to the man who is actually in the arena, whose face is marred by dust and sweat and blood; who strives valiantly; who errs, who comes short again and again, because there is no effort without error and shortcoming; but who does actually strive to do the deeds; who knows great enthusiasms, the great devotions; who spends himself in a worthy cause; who at the best knows in the end the triumph of high achievement, and who at the worst, if he fails, at least fails while daring greatly, so that his place shall never be with those cold and timid souls who neither know victory nor defeat."

- Theodore Roosevelt

CONTENTS

Welcome to This Guide ix

INTRODUCTION 11
   What is Cooling? 13
   Understanding Cooling – A Primer 14
      Temperature 14
      Heat 15
      Humidity 25
      Pressure 31
      Flow Rate 33
      Computation Fluid Dynamics (CFD) 38

COOLING SOURCES 41
   Refrigeration cycle 41
   Cooling Systems 47
      Computer Room Air Conditioner (CRAC) 47
      Computer Room Air Handler (CRAH) 48
      Direct Expansion (DX) Systems 49
      Glycol-cooled Systems 51
      Water-cooled Systems 53
      Chilled Water Systems 55
      Adiabatic Cooling 57
      Free Cooling or Economization 60

    Geothermal Cooling 63

    Immersion Cooling 65

    Liquid Cooling to the CPU 66

COOLING DISTRIBUTION 68

  Room Cooling 68

    7-Tile Pitch Rule 70

  Row Cooling 71

  Rack Cooling 72

  Cooling Path Elements 73

    Pump 73

    Pipe 74

    Isolators and Fittings 76

DETERMINING THE NEED 77

  The Concept of N 77

  Calculating N 78

    Heat Sources 79

    Air Flow 86

    Refrigerant Lines 91

    Water Lines 92

    Redundancy 96

    Tier Specification 96

COOLING EFFICIENCY 100

  The Need for Efficiency 100

    Cooling Efficiency Metrics 103
        Rack Cooling Index (RCI)® 103
        Return Temperature Index (RTI)™ 108
        Performance Indicator (PI) 110
        Water Usage Effectiveness (WUE) 114
    Cooling Efficiency Best Practices 116
        Aisle Arrangement 116
        Aisle Containment 117
        Sealed Rooms 118
        Airflow Management 118
        Cable Management 118
        Equipment Inlet Temperature/Humidity Adjustments 119
        Variable Speed Fan Drives (VSD) 120
        Air-Side and Water-Side Economizers 120

CODES AND STANDARDS 122
    Uptime Institute 122
    TIA 123
    BICSI 124
    ASHRAE 125
    ETSI 126
    NEBS 127

TEN-STEP FRAMEWORK 130

    The Ten Steps.. 130
    Case Study... 135
NEXT STEPS.. 136
BIBLIOGRAPHY... 137

Welcome to This Guide

If you are reading these words, it means you are interested in designing cooling systems for the Data Center. I welcome you to a rich trove of information.

Perhaps you have come here after reading my first guide – **Data Center for Beginners: A beginner's guide towards understanding Data Center Design**[1], and have decided to master the art of Data Center Design. Or you may be a newbie perching on this nest by chance. You may even be an experienced Data Center professional wishing to sharpen your craft. Regardless, you will find the information contained herein quite useful.

This guide is dedicated to studying the nitty-gritty of designing Cooling for the Data Center. I have attempted a direct approach devoid of flowery equivocation, aimed at giving you a firm foundation in your Data Center design career.

As an industry veteran, this is the guide I needed when I first started designing data center cooling systems. I trust you will share the same sentiment as well.

I hope it proves to be a valuable companion as you take your career to the next level.

Sincerely yours

B. A. Ayomaya

---

[1] Available on Amazon in Kindle and Paperback editions.

CHAPTER ONE

INTRODUCTION

In today's connected world, businesses more than ever need to, and are, relying on technology to achieve their objectives. The need for IT permeates the entire fabric of the modern enterprise. The way businesses produce, distribute, communicate, support, and deliver goods and services to their internal and external customers is heavily reliant on IT. This profound dependence predicates the importance of the Data Center.

The Data Center exists to enable the business' IT needs. Businesses realize their IT needs by running applications on Servers, saving data on Storage, and sharing information through Networks. These IT building blocks are set up and operated on in the Data Center.

One of the most critical aspects of the Data Center is cooling. Cooling accounts for up to 20% of the Data Center requirements.

The IT equipment, through which business objectives are realized, and for which the data center is constructed, require optimal environmental conditions to perform properly. Above certain temperatures, these equipment will not function, and may well get damaged. Cooling the data center environment is vital to realizing business objectives.

INTRODUCTION

The above is to underscore how important the understanding of Cooling and all its aspects - generation, distribution, and delivery – is to you, the budding Data Center designer. The subsequent pages will help you on this journey.

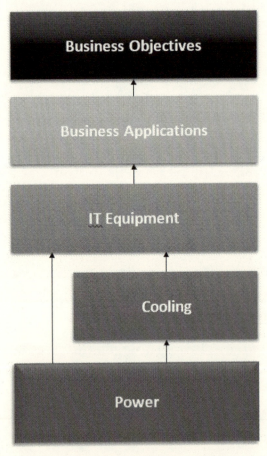

The Data Center Value Chain

What is Cooling?

Cooling is the process of making a place, or a thing, colder. In technical parlance, cooling is the transfer of heat from a substance of higher temperature to another substance of lower temperature. The substance hitherto with higher temperature becomes colder, while that originally with a lower temperature becomes hotter.

As far as the data center is concerned, the objective is to remove heat from the data center space to the external environment and maintain conducive conditions for the optimal functioning of the data center equipment.

We learn from the Law of Conservation of Energy, that energy cannot be created or destroyed in an isolated system, but can be transformed from one form to another. When electrical equipment uses power, the electrical energy consumed becomes transformed to heat energy. This heat is discharged into the data center environment. Since the room is enclosed, the heat builds up, leading to a steady rise in the room temperatures. The purpose of data center cooling is to remove this heat in an efficient manner. The data center designer must ensure that sufficient cooling is available to IT equipment in the data center as long as they are powered up.

Despite the critical nature of data center cooling, it remains one of the least understood aspects of data center design. Most designers focus on providing reliable power

INTRODUCTION

to the environment and simply place cooling units in the room. The effect is a proliferation of cooling equipment thus adding more strain to the power requirements and operational efficiency metrics.

Understanding Cooling – A Primer

Understanding cooling will require familiarization with some concepts. It might still be helpful though to consult other sources if necessary.

Temperature

Temperature is a property of a substance that is used to determine how hot, or how cold, the substance is, measured in terms of well-defined scales. There are three common scales in use today – the Celsius scale (ºC), the Fahrenheit scale (ºF), and the Kelvin scale (K). Of these three, the Celsius scale is the most common.

An object's temperature is determined by the rate of movement, or kinetic energy, of its atoms and molecules. Boiling water has molecules moving at a faster rate than those of iced water, thus a temperature difference.

Temperature measures the average kinetic energy of the atoms and molecules of a substance.

It is important to note that, although related, temperature and heat are distinctly different. While heat is a form of energy, temperature is a physical property of an object.

Temperature is measured by a device known as the thermometer. The thermometer consists of a mechanism to sense changes in temperature, and the means to express these changes in numerical value. A common way of sensing temperature is to place some mercury is a glass bulb attached to a narrow glass tube, as occurs in the mercury-in-glass thermometer.

As temperature changes, the volume of the mercury changes slightly, and is driven along the narrow tube. The distance of travel is measured to determine the temperature change.

Mercury Thermometer

Heat

Heat is a form of energy that is transferred from one substance to another as a result of a difference in temperatures. Heat is transferred from substance A with a higher temperature to substance B with a lower temperature. As a result of this transference, substance A would typically have a lower temperature, while substance B has a higher temperature.

INTRODUCTION 16

Kinetic energy in the atoms or molecules in substance A gets converted to the flowing heat energy, thus bringing down its temperature.

If substance A and substance B are of the same temperature, no heat will flow.

It is important to note that heat is not a quality of either substance A or B. Heat is a form of energy that flows. It is a result of the two substances coming in contact, and cannot exist in the absence of either.

As heat is a form of energy, it is measured in Joules (J). Heat is also measured in British Thermal Unit (BTU) and Calories. However, in designing cooling for the data center, we are mostly concerned with the *heat rate*. The heat rate is analogous to *power* in electrical systems. While power is the rate, per time, at which electrical energy is transferred, heat rate is the rate, per time, at which heat energy is transferred. Both heat rate and power are measured in Watts (W).

Heat rate is the rate, per time, at which heat energy is transferred from one substance to another.

The total power consumed by the electrical equipment in the data center equals the rate at which heat is discharged to the surrounding environment since all electrical energy is eventually converted to heat energy. Hence, the heat needs to be removed at a similar or faster rate to prevent building up heat in the room, leading to a rise in temperature.

Heat Capacity

Unlike heat, which is a form of energy in transit, heat capacity is an intrinsic property of an object. An object's heat capacity is the amount of heat required to change its temperature by a certain amount. Heat capacity measures the resistance of an object to changes in its temperature.

Heat capacity is dependent on the size of the object. The amount of heat required to increase the temperature of 2kg of an object is twice that required for only 1kg of the object. For comparison between objects, a more accurate measure is the *specific heat capacity* or simply specific heat.

Specific heat capacity is the amount of heat required to change the temperature of a unit mass of an object by a unit temperature (one degree Celsius or one degree Kelvin) without any change in phase. Specific heat capacity is the heat capacity per unit mass of an object.

This relationship is depicted by the equation

$$Q = mc\Delta T$$

Where

Q = the measured heat that caused the object's rise in temperature

INTRODUCTION

m = the mass of the object

c = the specific heat capacity of the object

ΔT = the change in temperature, which for our purpose 1K or 1°C

Specific heat capacity is measured in J/kg°C or J/kgK. The specific heat capacities of several materials have been measured and are available in literature.

Thus, if we know the specific heat capacity of an object (c), its mass (m), its change in temperature after heat is applied or removed (ΔT), and the length of time in which the heat is applied or removed (t), we can determine the heat rate using the following equation:

$$Heat\ rate = \frac{mc\Delta T}{t}$$

This is useful when computing the cooling requirements of the data center.

Heat Transfer

Heat is energy in transit, transferred from one substance to another. There are three fundamental ways by which this transference occurs – Conduction, Convection, and Radiation.

Conduction occurs when two bodies with varying temperatures come in direct contact with one another. The excited molecules and electrons in the substance with a higher temperature transfer some of their energy to the adjacent molecules and electrons, thereby causing heat to flow.

Substances that are easily receptive to this transfer of energy so that heat flows through them effortlessly are said to be good heat conductors. They have large thermal conductivities. Metals are very good conductors of heat.

Conduction usually occurs in solids or stationary fluids.

Convection is the means through which heat is transferred from a hot place to a cold place.

Convection occurs in moving liquids or gases. A liquid or gas with a high temperature weighs less than the same volume of such liquid or gas. Therefore the lighter liquid or gas moves faster and rises, with the vacated spaces filled by the colder and heavier liquid or gas.

In the data center, the room is heated and cooled through convection. Heat discharged from the electrical equipment is conducted into the surrounding air. The resultant hot air rises and displaces the colder air around it. This

INTRODUCTION 20

pattern continues until the room is filled with hot air. Cooling occurs by continuously removing some hot air and replacing it with cold air until the room is filled with cold air.

As long as the electrical equipment keep working, there will always be hot air. Therefore, cold air needs to be introduced at an equal or faster rate than that at which the air is heated.

Radiation occurs when heat is transferred from between two objects, or from one place to another, without any contact or intermediary.

When an object is being heated, the increased excitation of molecules and charged particles generate electromagnetic radiation. The radiation is discharged in all directions at the speed of light and can travel through empty space until it is absorbed by other substances. Upon absorption, energy is released and the other substances are heated up.

An example of radiation is the heating of the earth by the sun. The earth's surface, and all objects on it, absorb radiated energy from the sun and thus become of a higher temperature.

Radiation is sometimes visible, depending on its wavelength. An example is the bluish, yellowish, and sometimes reddish glow of a burning flame. The difference in colors is a result of the difference in energy radiated by the heated particles.

The rate at which a substance absorbs the radiated energy depends on the nature of its surface. A black surface is an excellent absorber of radiation. Therefore, the blacker the surface of the substance, the more radiation it absorbs.

Thermal Conductivity

Thermal conductivity is the ability of a material to conduct heat. It is heat conducted per unit length of the material. A high thermal conductivity means that heat transfer across a material will occur at a high rate.

Thermal conductivity is also known as k-value or λ-value. The units of thermal conductivity are W/m·K.

The thermal conductivities for several materials have been measured and are available in literature.

Thermal Insulance

Thermal insulance is the ability of a material to resist heat flow. Thermal insulance is also known as R-value. The units of thermal insulance are m²·K/W.

Thermal insulance is calculated by dividing the material thickness by the material's thermal conductivity.

INTRODUCTION

$$R-value = \frac{Material\ Thickness\ (m)}{Material\ Thermal\ Conductivity\ (W/m.K)}$$

The R-value of an object that is a composite of several materials is the sum of the R-values of each material that make up the object.

Consider a cavity wall composed of the following layers:

- Inner surface resistance
- 10mm clay bricks
- 5mm glass wool
- 10mm concrete blocks
- Outside surface resistance

The overall R-value of the cavity wall is computed as follows:

Material	Thickness (m)	k-value (W/m·K)	R-value (K·m²/W)
Inner surface resistance	N/A	N/A	0.04
Clay bricks	0.10m	0.77	0.13
Glass wool	0.05m	0.04	1.25
Concrete blocks	0.10m	1.13	0.09
Surface Resistance	N/A		0.13
OVERALL R-VALUE			**1.64**

Thermal Transmittance

Thermal transmittance is the reciprocal of thermal insulance. Also known as the U-value, thermal transmittance is the rate of transfer of heat through a structure divided by the difference in temperature across that structure. The units of measurement are W/m²K.

The lower the U-value of a structure, the better-insulated the structure is. The installation must avoid other possible openings and gaps as this could considerably increase the thermal transmittance.

In our sample cavity wall above, the thermal transmittance is computed as follows:

$$U-value = \frac{1}{R-value} = \frac{1}{1.64}$$
$$= 0.61 W/m^2K$$

Object Phases

When an object absorbs heat from another object, it typically experiences a rise in temperature. However, this is not always the case. This is because objects exist in one of three physical states – solid form, liquid form, or gaseous form. When enough heat is absorbed, this heat causes the object to change its physical state from one form to another.

INTRODUCTION

When an object changes its state from a solid form to a liquid form, the object is said to *melt*. The temperature at which this change occurs is called the *melting point*.

When an object changes its state from a liquid form to a gaseous form, the object is said to *boil*. The temperature at which this change occurs is called the *boiling point*.

Sometimes, the heat can be so great as to cause the direct change of an object from a solid form to a gaseous form, without melting. This phenomenon, known as *sublimation* occurs as a result of an interplay of temperature with other variables, such as pressure. The temperature at which this occurs is called the *sublimation temperature*.

The process of an object changing to its gaseous form, either by boiling or sublimation, is known as *vaporization*.

An object in its liquid form can also change into its gaseous form without reaching its boiling point. This is known as *evaporation*.

Sensible Heat and Latent Heat

As absorption of heat can either cause an object's rise in temperature or change in physical state, a distinction is needed between these two reactions.

Heat that effects only a change in temperature known as *sensible heat*.

Heat that effects only a change in physical state, without any further rise in temperature, is known as *latent heat*.

An object can absorb both latent heat and sensible heat. Consider a liquid at a temperature below its boiling point. If heat is applied to it, its temperature rises until the liquid boils and vaporizes to its gaseous form. The moment at which the vaporization occurs, the gaseous form has exactly the same temperature as the liquid's boiling point temperature. Therefore, the total heat absorbed by the liquid is a combination of the sensible heat needed to raise its temperature, and the latent heat needed to convert its state.

We mentioned before that in evaporation, a liquid can become gaseous without boiling. During evaporation, only a small portion of the liquid becomes gaseous. The latent heat needed to transform that small portion into gas is absorbed from the sensible heat of the remaining body of the liquid. As a result, the liquid that does not evaporate becomes cooler.

Evaporation can occur at any temperature and pressure.

Humidity

Our planet is filled with water. Over 70% of the earth's surface is covered by water. Water is also found in homes and workplaces employed for a variety of uses.

INTRODUCTION

Some of this water will eventually evaporate or change phase into its gaseous state and get absorbed by the air in the atmosphere. This gaseous state of water is called water vapor.

Humidity is a measure of the amount of water vapor present in the air. The higher the humidity, the higher the presence of water vapor in the air, and vice versa. A high level of humidity poses a problem to the human body and the IT equipment, as it indicates that there is little room for more water vapor in the given volume of air present.

The human body tries to regulate its temperature through the process of sweating. When one sweats, heat transfers from the body to the sweat, thus causing the body to cool. The sweat water eventually evaporates. The sweat-turn-water vapor tries to get absorbed into the atmosphere. If the humidity level is high, there will be no space for new amounts of water vapor, causing the swampy feeling of sweat stuck in your cloth and body.

For IT equipment, high humidity is also a problem. When the equipment room is cooled, the water vapor in the air can get condensed back into liquid water which can damage the equipment.

Absolute and Relative Humidity

We have seen that humidity is the quantity of water vapor in the air. When the actual mass of water vapor in a volume of air is measured and quantified, we refer to this as absolute humidity.

Absolute humidity is measured in grams per cubic meter (g/m³).

$$Absolute\ Humidity = \frac{Mass\ of\ Water\ Vapor}{Volume\ of\ Air}$$

A more common way of measuring humidity however is the concept of relative humidity.

Relative humidity is the ratio of the current absolute humidity to the maximum possible absolute humidity at a given temperature, expressed as a percentage.

$$Relative\ Humidity = \frac{Current\ Absolute\ Humidity}{Maximum\ Possible\ Absolute\ Humidity} \times 100\%$$

A relative humidity of 100% means that the air is fully saturated and is no longer able to hold more water vapor.

The human body feels more comfortable at a relative humidity of 45%. A relative humidity of 40% - 60% is ideal for IT equipment rooms.

Dew Point

Relative humidity can change depending on the current temperature. As air temperature rises, the molecules in the air have more freedom to move, giving more space for water vapor and lower relative humidity. The reverse is the case when air temperature drops and relative humidity rises.

The temperature at which relative humidity rises to 100% is known as the *dew point*. This is because if the temperature goes any lower, the water vapor in the atmosphere will begin to condense.

The knowledge of the dew point is critical for IT equipment rooms. It helps operators realize how far they need to manipulate temperatures to maintain the proper operation of IT equipment.

Dry Bulb and Wet Bulb Temperatures

Another way to determine the state of humidity in the air is the concept of the dry-bulb and wet-bulb temperatures.

When the thermometer measures the temperature of dry air, without any impact of moisture or water vapor present in the air, the measured temperature is known as the *dry-bulb temperature*, indicating that the thermometer bulb is completely dry.

The dry-bulb temperature is taken by shielding the thermometer from air and radiation, then exposing it freely to air.

The dry-bulb temperature is the ambient temperature of the air.

We have explained before that evaporation of water cools the surface where the water hitherto was. If the water is present in the air, its evaporation will cool the surrounding air.

The wet-bulb temperature is the lowest possible temperature to which air can be cooled at constant pressure as a result of the evaporation of water.

The wet-bulb temperature is taken by wrapping the thermometer bulb with wet muslin to keep it moist, then exposing it freely to air. However, it is kept free from radiation. The measured temperature is the wet-bulb temperature.

The wet-bulb temperature is always lower or equal to the dry-bulb temperature. When humidity is high, less water gets to evaporate so that wet-bulb temperature is closer to the dry-bulb temperature.

When the dry-bulb temperature equals the dew point temperature, the dry-bulb temperature and the wet-bulb temperature are the same.

Therefore, at 100% relative humidity,

INTRODUCTION

Dry-bulb temperature = Wet-bulb temperature
= Dew point temperature

Psychrometric Chart

Psychometrics is the study of the physical and thermodynamic properties of gas-vapor mixtures.

The psychrometric chart is a graph that shows the thermodynamic properties of humid air. The properties are measured at constant pressure and a given elevation relative to the sea level. Thermodynamic properties include dry bulb temperature (DBT), wet bulb temperature (WBT), dew point temperature (DPT), relative humidity (RH), humidity ration, humid air volume, and enthalpy.

Learning how to read the psychometric graph is beyond the scope of this book.

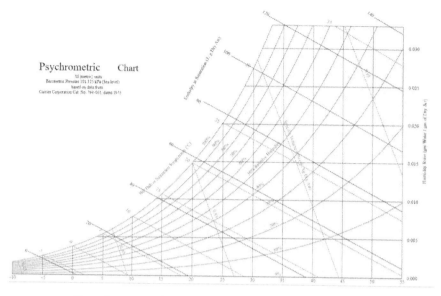

Psychrometric chart (Author: Arthur Ogawa)

Pressure

Pressure is a quantity that measures the amount of force applied perpendicular to a unit area.

When force is applied to a surface, the force is evenly distributed across the area of the surface. Pressure is the total concentrated force applied to each square meter of the surface area.

$$Pressure = \frac{Total\ Applied\ Force}{Surface\ Area}$$

INTRODUCTION

The standard unit for measuring pressure is Pascal (Pa). A unit pascal is the pressure measured when one unit of force is applied to a surface area of one square meter.

$$1Pa = \frac{1N}{1m^2}$$

In addition to solids, fluids - liquids and gases - also apply pressure. This pressure stems from the pull of gravity on the fluid and increases with the mass of the fluid. It follows also that a greater volume of fluid exerts a larger amount of pressure.

The longer the depth of the fluid, the greater the pressure exerted on the surface below it. Therefore, as the surface moves to a higher elevation, the pressure reduces. This is why the pressure from the atmosphere reduces on airplanes as they rise.

Relationship between Pressure and Temperature

Consider a fluid sealed in a container, so that none of it is allowed to escape, and nothing is allowed to come into the container, the total volume of space the fluid can fill is fixed and limited.

If pressure is applied to the fluid in this fixed volume, the kinetic energy of the fluid's atoms and molecules increases, causing the temperature to rise. An expansion of the volume will allow the atoms and molecules to escape, reducing kinetic energy and eventually the temperature.

Therefore, as long as the volume is kept constant, pressure and temperature have a direct relationship. An increase in pressure causes a simultaneous increase in temperature. The reverse is also the case.

These changes in temperature can also bring about a phase change in the fluid so that it changes from liquid to gas, or gas to liquid.

Flow Rate

Consider a volume of fluid present in a medium, say a pipe, that pressure has applied to so that it flows in a particular direction.

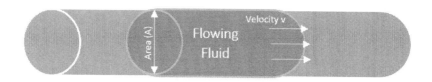

As the fluid flows from one end of the pipe to the other, we say the fluid is flowing at a certain *flow rate*. Flow rate is measured in m^3/s.

INTRODUCTION

The flow rate of a fluid is the volume of that fluid passing an area at a point in time

$$Flow\ Rate = \frac{Volume\ of\ Fluid\ Flowing}{Time\ it\ takes\ to\ flow}$$

If the velocity at which the liquid is flowing can be measured, the flow rate can also be determined by the following equation.

$$Flow\ Rate = Pipe\ Cross\text{-}sectional\ Area \times Velocity\ of\ Flow$$

This equation also applies if the fluid is in a gaseous state such as air. Assume we have a duct from which air is blowing, and the velocity at which the air flows is known. We can determine the flow rate by multiplying the duct's cross-sectional area by the velocity with which the air flows.

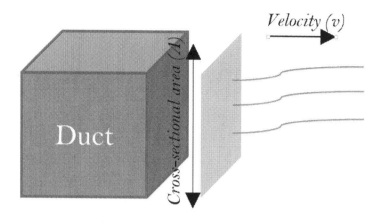

Air Flow Rate
   = Duct Cross-sectional Area
   × Velocity of Flow

Incompressible Fluids

Incompressible fluids, as the name implies, are fluids that cannot be compressed or squeezed to fit a certain space, so that they maintain the same volume at all times. Liquids are generally mostly incompressible.

Therefore, if liquids flow through a pipe, they must always maintain the same volume at all times. It follows that, at every section of the pipe, the flow rate is the same regardless of the shape of the pipe at the different points, as long as there are no impeding forces or pressures.

INTRODUCTION

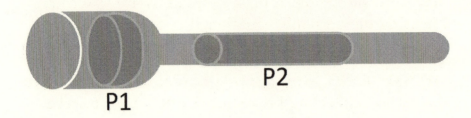

In the pipe above, the volume of the fluid at P1 is the same as the volume at P2. Likewise, the flow rates are the same.

Flow Rate at P1 = Flow Rate at P2

This is known as the equation of continuity. With this knowledge, we can surmise that in a pipe with two open ends, the flow rate with which a fluid enters one end of the pipe is the same as that with which it exits.

This knowledge is needed when computing requirements for removing heat from the room through the movement of fluids. If we know the volume of a fluid needed to absorb heat from the room while maintaining a certain temperature threshold, and the speed with which the heat must be removed from the room to maintain the room temperature, we can determine the sizing of the medium through which the fluid will flow.

However, how do we calculate the pressure required to force the fluid to flow at the required flow rate? We do this using the Bernoulli equation.

The equation recognizes that apart from the intended flow rate, the density of the fluid and effects of gravity are other factors affecting the required amount of pressure. The equation is as follows:

$$P_1 + \frac{1}{2}\rho v_1^2 + \rho g h_1 = P_2 + \frac{1}{2}\rho v_2^2 + \rho g h_2$$

Where,

P_1 = Pressure of the fluid at Point P1 in the Pipe

P_2 = Pressure of the fluid at Point P2 in the Pipe

v_1 = Velocity of the fluid at Point P1 in the Pipe

v_2 = Velocity of the fluid at Point P2 in the Pipe

h_1 = Height of the pipe from a reference point, say the ground, at Point P1

h_2 = Height of the pipe from a reference point, say the ground, at Point P2

ρ = Density of the fluid

g = Acceleration due the pull of gravity

INTRODUCTION

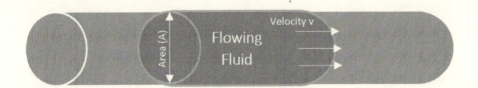

If an incompressible fluid flows through a streamlined, symmetric pipe without any variation in height at any point on the pipe as in the figure above, and no forces acting against the flow of the fluid, the pressure, velocity, and height will be the same at all points. Therefore, the Bernoulli equation can be rewritten as follows:

$$P + \frac{1}{2}\rho v^2 + \rho g h = constant$$

This constant will be the same at every point on the pipe.

Computation Fluid Dynamics (CFD)

Computation Fluid Dynamics (CFD) is a science derived from the field of Field Mechanics. CFD involves the analysis, simulation, and visualization of the flow of fluids given varying conditions. CFD achieves this through the use of complex numerical analysis and data structures.

CFD Modelling is useful in designing cooling systems for the data center. It enables the designer to visualize probable airflow distribution at different parameter values, allowing the optimal combination of these parameters and total cost-efficiency. These parameters include the supply air temperature and supply flow rate.

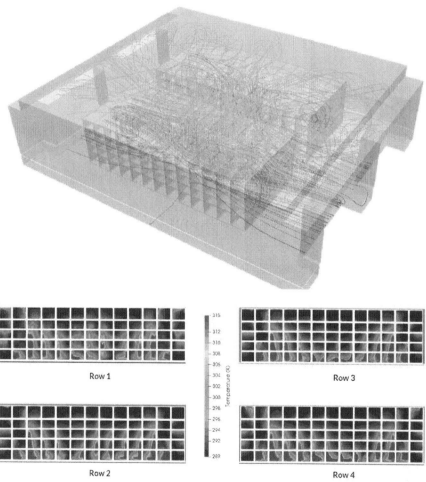

Data Center CFD Model (Source: SimScale)

INTRODUCTION

These visual models predict the pattern of airflow from the cooling units, the hot air discharged from the servers, and the hot and cold spots in the room.

With these, the designers can optimize the placement of cooling units and equipment racks layout for maximum cooling performance.

CHAPTER TWO
COOLING SOURCES

From the foregoing, we now have a fair understanding of what Cooling is. We also have a fair understanding of important concepts related to Cooling. Our attention now turns to sources from which Data Centers get their Cooling.

As explained in Chapter One, it is more accurate to say "removing heat" rather than "producing cooling". This is because hot air is taken from the room and returned to the room as cold air. Heat is removed from the hot air and discharged into the atmosphere until the temperature is as low as desired, after which it is supplied back to the room. As a result, the total volume of the air remains constant.

Heat is removed from the room through a process known as the Refrigeration Cycle.

Refrigeration cycle

The refrigeration cycle is the basic cooling principle common in all cooling systems. It occurs by moving a chemical compound, called the refrigerant, across different stages in a cycle. The resultant effect is heat being transferred from the cooled area to the outside environment.

COOLING SOURCES

The refrigerant is a substance that easily changes its state from liquid to gas and back again by absorbing heat from the environment. The most common refrigerants are Chlorofluorocarbons (CFCs), Hydrochlorofluorocarbons (HCFCs), and Hydrofluorocarbons (HFCs).

Refrigerant

The cooling unit collects hot air from the room. The refrigerant absorbs the heat from the hot air and discharges it to the outside environment via the refrigeration cycle.

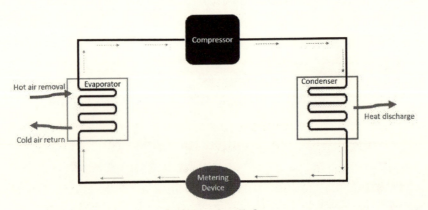

Refrigeration Cycle

The cycle begins with the Compressor. As the name implies, the compressor sucks in the refrigerant and compresses it. This process increases the pressure on the refrigerant. We know that increasing the pressure on a fluid while keeping its volume constant will increase the fluid's temperature. Thus the refrigerant leaves the compressor as a high-pressure, high-temperature gas.

Compressor (Source: Trane)

There are five main types of compressors used in the refrigeration industry. These are:

1. Reciprocating compressor
2. Rotary compressor
3. Scroll compressor
4. Screw compressor
5. Centrifugal compressor

In data center applications, however, the scroll compressor is mostly used. This is because of its modulating characteristics. With scroll technology, a

COOLING SOURCES

compressor can operate at a rate less than its full capacity. This is a significant development for energy efficiency, as the compressor consumes the most energy in a cooling system.

There are two main types of scroll compressors – the digital scroll compressor and the variable-speed compressor. The digital scroll compressor uses an SCR-based control system to disengage the top of the scroll when modulation is needed. The speed of the motor is always constant. The variable-speed compressor however achieves modulation by actually changing the speed of the motor using an inverter or a variable-frequency drive.

Both scroll compressor types achieve the same outcome and are widely used in many field applications, although the data center industry tends more to variable-speed types.

At the second stage, the refrigerant is passed to the Condenser. A fan blows over the condenser coil as the refrigerant moves along. We know that heat flows from the region of high temperature to that of low temperature. Via conduction, heat is passed onto the body of the coil from the high-temperature gas. The blown air will now have a lower temperature than the coil. It absorbs heat from the coil via convection and discharges it into the atmosphere.

The heat removed from the hitherto high-temperature gas causes it to condense into a liquid. However, the liquid is still of high-pressure and high-temperature.

Condenser (Source: Schneider Electric)

At the third stage of the cycle, the refrigerant is passed to a metering device. This device is also called an Expansion Valve. This device regulates the pressure of the on-rushing fluid before it moves over to the next stage of the cycle.

The reduction in pressure also causes a reduction in the refrigerant's temperature.

Thermostatic Expansion Valve

COOLING SOURCES

At the fourth stage, the refrigerant is now a low-pressure, low-temperature liquid. The refrigerant flows along to the Evaporator. Like the compressor, the evaporator also has a fan and a coil.

The evaporator sucks in hot air from the room to be cooled. The evaporator fan blows this air over the evaporator coil as the refrigerant moves along the coil. Since the air has a higher temperature, the liquid refrigerant absorbs heat from the air. This latent heat converts the refrigerant back to a cold gas as it leaves the evaporator, while the now cold air is blown back into the room. The cycle then resumes all over again.

Evaporator

Since evaporation is the last stage in the refrigeration cycle, there is a little delay before cold air is released into the room.

Cooling Systems

There are two broad systems through which heat collected from the room is ejected to the atmosphere. The cooling unit either directly takes the heat outside, or it redirects the heat to a central collector which then discharges the heat.

When heat is directly discharged, the cooling unit in the computer room is called a Computer Room Air Conditioner (CRAC). When heat is indirectly discharged, the cooling unit in the room is called a Computer Room Air Handler (CRAH) or Air Handling Unit (AHU).

Computer Room Air Conditioner (CRAC)

The CRAC is a device that collects heat from the data center and directly discharges to the atmosphere via some heat rejection medium.

CRAC (Source: Vertiv)

COOLING SOURCES

To achieve this, some of the components of the refrigeration cycle, are contained in the CRAC. Typically, these include the compressor, the evaporator, and the metering device. The condenser is located elsewhere.

CRAC-based systems are the most common approach for cooling data centers. They are suitable for use with data centers of any size.

Computer Room Air Handler (CRAH)

The CRAH is similar to appearance with the CRAC but works differently. It collects heat from the data center and redirects it to a central cooling system, typically a Chiller.

All the components of the refrigeration cycle are contained in the central cooling system. When used with a Chiller, the CRAH cools the room by drawing hot air and blowing it over a coil where chilled water from the Chiller flows. The chilled water absorbs the heat and carries it to the Chiller so that the refrigeration cycle commences.

CRAH (Source: Schneider Electric)

Direct Expansion (DX) Systems

Direct Expansion (DX) Systems are the most common form of cooling found in data centers. They are compatible with data centers of all forms and sizes. They are also easy to design, install, and maintain.

In a DX System, the CRAC contains some of the components of the refrigeration cycle. The other components are located outdoors. The refrigerant moves between the indoor and outdoor components through connecting pipes known as refrigerant lines.

COOLING SOURCES

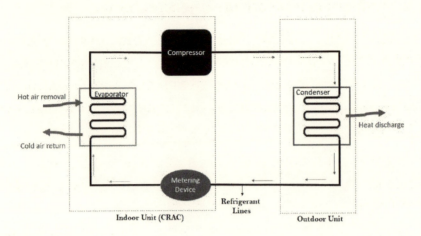

DX System

The system is called a Split System when half of the components of the refrigeration cycle are located outside and the other half are located inside. In a Split System, the condenser and the compressor are usually outside.

DX Systems are also qualified as 'air-cooled' systems because the heat is absorbed from the refrigerant by the movement of air around the condenser coils.

A drawback of DX Systems is that refrigerant lines need to be properly engineered to allow the refrigerant to move as much heat as intended. Changes in height and cross-sectional areas affect the refrigerant pressure. There is also a limit to the allowed distances between the indoor and outdoor units before inefficiencies set in.

However, some DX systems have all components of the refrigerant cycle self-contained in a single enclosure. As there is no need for any piping for refrigerant flow, these systems are usually mounted through the wall or window, with the condenser section facing outside.

In some installations, the entire unit is in the IT room while air into and out of the condensing unit are ducted from outside.

Self-contained DX systems are most used in facilities will low capacity requirements.

Glycol-cooled Systems

In glycol-cooled systems, heat is removed from the refrigerant through the use of glycol. Glycol is a mixture of water and ethylene glycol.

By using flowing glycol instead, glycol-cooled systems replace the need in air-cooled DX systems for the refrigerant flowing outside to the condenser.

Similar to self-contained DX systems, glycol-cooled systems have all the components of the refrigeration cycle located inside the CRAC. However, instead of condensing coils, glycol-cooled systems use heat exchangers.

COOLING SOURCES

A volume of glycol absorbs much more heat than air of the same volume. It can also transport heat at a faster rate than air. Thus the heat exchanger is a lot smaller than the typical condenser.

The heat exchanger passes the heat from the refrigerant into glycol, which then flows through pipes outdoors to a fluid cooler. The heat in the warm glycol is then transferred to air in the atmosphere.

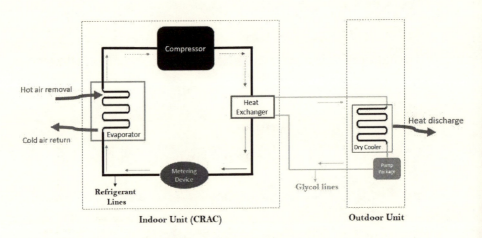

Glycol-Cooled System

Glycol can run much further than refrigerant pipes. However, pumps and valves are required to modulate the flow rate and circulate the glycol along the glycol lines. . Multiple CRACs can use a single fluid cooler and pump package.

Although more efficient than traditional air-cooled systems, glycol-cooled systems add additional layers of complexity. The glycol fluid in the IT space presents a risk. Also, the entire glycol system – pump package, fluid cooler, glycol lines, etc, have to be maintained.

Water-cooled Systems

Water-cooled systems are very similar to glycol-cooled systems. All components of the refrigeration cycle are integrated into the CRAC, with the heat exchanger replacing the condenser. However, instead of glycol, water is used to remove the hot air from the environment.

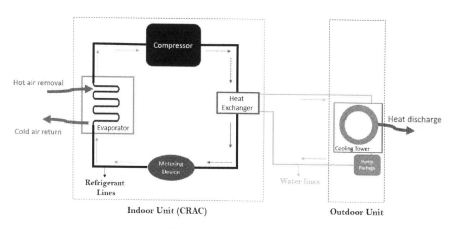

Water-Cooled System

In addition, water-cooled systems use a cooling tower instead of a dry cooler to reject the heat into the

COOLING SOURCES

atmosphere. Multiple CRAC units can be serviced by a single cooling tower.

A cooling tower works on the principle of evaporative cooling. When water evaporates, the latent heat causing the evaporation is absorbed from the environment, leading to lower surrounding temperatures.

When warm water arrives at the cooling tower from the CRAC, it is spread around a material, called the fill, on top of the tower. The spread water begins to drip down to the bottom of the tower. Along the way, some of the water evaporates, so that the rest of the water is cooled down. The cold water is collected at the cooling tower basin and sent back to the CRAC via the pump package.

At the same time, the cooling tower fans suck air upwards into the tower. The air serves to accelerate the evaporation and then rises to be discharged out into the atmosphere.

The evaporated water is called drift. Due to drift loss, some makeup water needs to be at hand to top up the water in the circuit when overly degraded by drift and other losses.

To reduce the quantity of water lost to drift, cooling towers have a component known as drift eliminator. When the sucked-in air comes in contact with drift, heat transfer occurs making some of the drift to condense. The drift eliminator catches the condensed droplets and sends them back to the cooling tower. This significantly reduces the quantity of water loss from the system.

There are different types of cooling towers depending on how draft is formed. Some of the more common are Counter Flow Induced Draft, Crossed Flow Induced Draft, and Counter Flow Forced Draft.

Chilled Water Systems

In a Chilled Water System, all components of the refrigeration cycle are centralized in a device called the water chiller, or chiller for short. The refrigeration cycle in the chiller produces chilled water, which is then pumped to flow through pipes to the Computer Room Air Handlers (CRAH) located in the computer rooms.

The CRAH transfers heat from the room into the chilled water. The now hot water is transferred back to the chiller for refrigeration and the cycle continues.

As with cooling towers, a body of makeup water needs to be kept in place. Chilled water lines can run for extensive distances. Some of the returning hot water is lost to evaporation. There might be some leakages around pipe joints. And, in some cases, contaminated water may need to be flushed out of the system.

Chilled water systems are generally more efficient than DX systems. They are also easier to maintain. However the initial capital outlay is quite substantial. Therefore,

COOLING SOURCES

capacity requirements need to substantial to justify the expenses.

Chilled water systems take up more space than DX system due complex pipe work. They are also more difficult to design and install. However, when properly installed, maintenance and repair works are minimal when compared to DX systems.

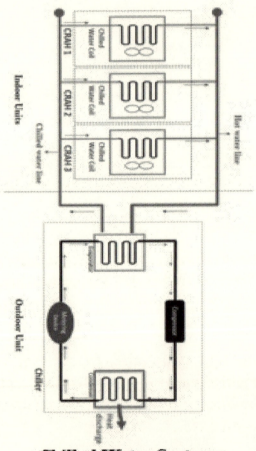

Chilled Water Systems

Like DX Systems, chilled water systems can be air-cooled, glycol-cooled, or water-cooled.

Air-cooled chillers reject heat by transferring heat directly to air. Air-cooled chillers are typically located outdoors.

Glycol-cooled chillers reject heat by transferring heat into glycol which then flows to a dry cooler for further heat rejection. Glycol-cooled chillers are typically located indoors.

Water-cooled chillers reject heat by transferring the heat into water which then flows to a cooling tower.

Adiabatic Cooling

Adiabatic cooling is the process of cooling without direct transfer of heat between systems. It is cooling without the addition, or removal, of energy.

The most common implementation of adiabatic cooling occurs in evaporative cooling. We discussed before that evaporative cooling occurs when water evaporates by removing sensible heat from its surroundings.

In adiabatic cooling, the hot air is passed over a wet damper or sprinkled water. This water evaporates thus cooling the air. There is no compression or interaction with refrigeration gases.

COOLING SOURCES

Adiabatic cooling can be direct or indirect. In direct adiabatic cooling, the hot air from the room is directly cooled by the evaporative process. However, the now cooler air will have a higher absolute humidity. There is also the risk of contamination from the water vapor.

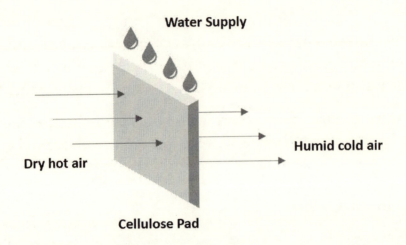

Direct Adiabatic Cooling

Therefore, direct adiabatic cooling is not suitable for data centers except in cases where humidification is desired.

Indirect adiabatic cooling on the other hand produces cool air without any humidification. The system contains two separated streams of air – the hot air from the data center, which is the secondary stream, and ambient air from the environment, which is the primary stream to be introduced to the environment.

The ambient air from the environment is passed through a filter to remove unwanted contaminants before being sent to the heat exchanger.

Simultaneously, the hot air from the data center is cooled via evaporative cooling then introduced into the heat exchanger.

In the heat exchanger, the cold humid air is used to cool the warmer ambient air from the environment. The now cooler ambient air is then supplied to the IT environment.

In some other implementations, the primary air stream is the hot air from the data center, while the secondary air stream that is cooled evaporatively is the ambient air stream.

Of course, this is a simple description of the system. In practice, the adiabatic cooling system needs to be carefully designed to produce the required cooling. When indirect adiabatic cooling is used, care must be taken to prevent pollution from ambient air.

Adiabatic cooling can become unfeasible in climates with higher relative humidity.

Variable Speed Drives

Variable speed drives (VSDs), also called adjustable speed drives (ASDs), are devices that can vary the speed of a normally fixed speed motor. They are used to control the speed of fans in the CRAC/CRAH, the pressure from

COOLING SOURCES

pumping stations, and the compressors in the chillers. This allows the cooling system operate at different capacities thus capturing energy savings.

Free Cooling or Economization

Data centers account for a high proportion of the world's energy usage. The prevalent ways through which we generate energy have an adverse effect on the environment. For the data center designer, efficiency in energy usage while keeping with capacity requirements is the desired outcome.

In a typical data center, cooling infrastructure gulps up to 40% of total energy usage. Innovative technologies continue to emerge through which the data center can be cooled at lower energy footprints.

One of such methods is leveraging nature itself. Datacenter cooling equipment makes use of natural phenomena to cool the datacenter so that there is less need to generate energy that would inadvertently pollute the environment.

These devices are called *Economizers*.

There are two main types of Economizers. These are Air-Side Economizers and Water-Side Economizers.

Air-Side Economizers

Air-side economizers work by utilizing outside air to direct cool the IT environment. This phenomenon is known as free-cooling.

When the temperature of the surrounding ambient air is sufficient to maintain the operation of the IT equipment, the air is simply treated to remove impurities, and then directly introduced into the IT environment. The hot air exhaust from the IT equipment is ducted outside to the surroundings.

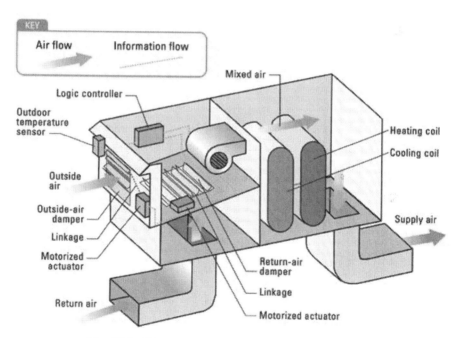

Air-Side Economizer (Source: EnergyStar)

COOLING SOURCES

When the outside air is very much below the required room temperature, some of the exhaust hot air is mixed with the collected outside air, and then supplied back to the room.

The air-side economizer is usually integrated into the CRAH for distribution to the IT equipment.

Air-side economization can be utilized in any region or environment in the world. However, the number of hours available for economization might differ. In hot climates, for instance, air-side economization can be used in the evenings when temperatures are lower, or in winter periods.

Air-side economization needs to be properly designed so as not to present additional problems. The outside air could be too dry thus necessitating humidification, or too humid hence requiring dehumidification. In addition, environmental particles and contaminants need to be properly filtered away. Another critical component is the sensing and control system which is very significant to the operation of the air-side economizer.

Water-Side Economizers

Similar to air-side economizers, water-side economizers utilize natural phenomena to provide cooling to the data center.

Water-side economization applies to chilled water systems. It works by producing chilled water directly from a cooling tower through evaporative cooling, thus bypassing the need for refrigeration by the chiller. Water-side economization provides additional resilience to the data center cooling system as the chiller can be by-passed completely.

Water-side economization produces huge savings in cooling operation. However, water-side economizers are best suited in climates where the wet-bulb temperature is lower than 55°F for 3,000 hours or more per year.

Similar to air-side economization, a critical component of water-side economization is the control system. The logic to switch from economization to refrigeration must be regularly certified to operate as intended. Also, Variable Speed Drives (VSDs) should be used with the cooling tower.

If the data center is designed to allow higher inlet temperatures into the IT racks, water-side economization can be used more often.

Geothermal Cooling

Geothermal Cooling is another method of cooling that aims to achieve energy efficiency utilizing natural phenomena.

COOLING SOURCES

Unlike ambient air temperatures which vary depending on climatic conditions, the temperature below the earth's surface remains mostly constant. This is due to the heat-insulating properties of the earth.

Geothermal cooling works by collecting heat from the room and channeling it into the cooler earth with or without the need for further refrigeration. All the components of the refrigeration cycle are located in the indoor CRAC/CRAH. However, the condenser is replaced by a closed-loop piping system that is channeled into the earth.

Water absorbs heat from the room either directly through a heat exchanger as in a CRAH, or indirectly from the refrigerant as in a CRAC. This warm water is pumped through the closed-loop piping system into the earth where it discharges the heat and returns as cold water. The cycle then resumes again.

Geothermal cooling presents the possibility for much energy savings and environmental conservation. In addition, the costs to maintain the installation are much less than conventional cooling systems.

A misconception about geothermal cooling is that it requires a lot of real-estate for the earth loop. However, there are four methods of creating the earth loop. At least one of those methods would be applicable regardless of the size of real-estate available.

Immersion Cooling

As more computing power continues to be packed into the data center equipment, heat generation will continue to rise. The industry therefore constantly engages in research to innovate better ways of cooling the data center. One of such ways is immersion cooling.

In immersion cooling, the heat-generating equipment is completely submerged in a circulating cooling liquid. This liquid must be *dielectric*, or insulating, so that it does not damage the circuit components when in contact. The coolant absorbs all of the heat and discharges it into water via a heat exchanger. The water then takes heat out of the room either to the environment via any of means previously discussed, or to the building for other uses.

Immersion Cooling (Source: GRC)

Liquid Cooling to the CPU

Another efficiency-seeking cooling approach is Liquid Cooling to the CPU. It is known that the processing components generally produce the most heat in IT equipment. If an efficient way can be developed to harvest heat directly from the CPU and other processing components such as the GPU, expensive whole room cooling systems can be eliminated. This will drastically reduce procurement and operational costs for both power and cooling.

In Liquid Cooling to the CPU, instead of air being the means of heat transfer from the CPU to the surroundings, liquid is used. Liquid generally transfers much more heat per volume than air.

Common implementations involve the processing unit being completely immersed in a sealed container filled with a special liquid coolant. The coolant transfers the heat to a heat exchanger. A pump system continuously circulates water to and from the heat exchanger. The circulating water removes heat from the room for other uses in the building. One of the better-known technology brands in this space is ICEOTOPE.

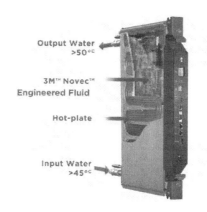

Iceotope Liquid Cooling

(Source: Data Center Knowledge)

CHAPTER THREE
COOLING DISTRIBUTION

In the preceding chapters, we saw that cooling is the removal of heat from the room. We also examined the various means through which heat is extracted and discharged.

The cold air reintroduced to the room via the CRAC/CRAH needs to be distributed to the areas where it is most needed. This chapter discusses the various approaches to air distribution.

Room Cooling

In room cooling, the CRAC/CRAH are designed with capacities to cool the entire room. There is no special way to direct the cold air to spaces with higher heat exhaust. The cooling system is equipped with vigorous cold/hot air mixers to bring the room to an equalized stable temperature.

The cooling units are placed in positions where they have the best chance to absorb the hot air. Most times, a CFD analysis is necessary to simulate the airflow. However, the cold air may not permeate the entire room, creating pockets of hot spots. Again hot air may circulate to the rack inlet leading to insufficient cooling where required.

To mediate against this, some room cooling implementations make use of raised floors. A false floor is erected over the actual floor so that there is a void in between. The cold air is discharged into this void and escapes to the room via perforated floor tiles. These tiles in front of racks and in places where cold air is required. When layout configurations change, the perforated tiles are relocated to the new hot spots.

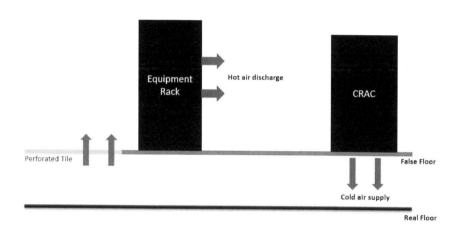

The air flow-rate through the average perforated tile typically does not allow for cooling of power densities beyond 4kW per rack.

Another approach is to directly channel the cold air to the cooled spaces through overhead ductwork. This allows for easy adjustments of air delivery in response to changing data center loads. However, it restricts flexibility in planning and rack layouts as ductworks cannot be easily modified after the data center goes live.

When using raised-floors for airflow management, it is best-practice for the void between the false and real floors to have a minimum height of 600mm, otherwise, overhead airflow should be utilized[2].

Room cooling architectures are difficult to adjust if cooling requirements change. Hence, cooling units are usually oversized to cater to estimated future needs. These estimations may and may not be correct. However, the relative simplicity of planning, costing, and implementation make it attractive to data center designers.

7-Tile Pitch Rule

To simplify airflow management in room cooling, the 7 Pitch Tile rule is utilized. The IT racks are arranged in rows such that the front and backs of adjacent rows face each other. This leads to a repeatable sequence after every 7 tiles, known as the 7-tile pitch rule.

Perforated tiles, or cold air ducts, are placed at the front of the racks. This channels the cold air to this location so that the aisle between rack fronts facing each other is distinctly cold, thus it is called a cold aisle. Conversely,

---

[2] Both overhead and underfloor distributions approaches have their pros and cons. Proper analysis should be made before selecting an option.

the aisle between rack backs becomes distinctly hot, hence it is called the hot aisle.

The cooling unit is placed at the hot aisle so that it easily absorbs the hot air.

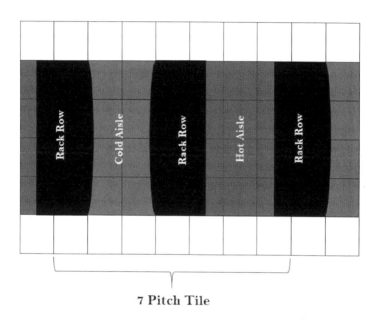

7 Pitch Tile

Row Cooling

In row cooling, the cooling units are placed in-row with the IT racks. The racks are laid out in rows and grouped by their power densities. This allows each row to run different load densities, so that differing cooling intensities can be applied as required. Differently sized

COOLING DISTRIBUTION

cooling units can be placed in-line with rows with corresponding heat removal requirements.

Hot-spot and cooling irregularities can be easily managed by proper layout and equipment placement. Besides, raised floors may not be needed thus saving cost.

This approach to cooling is flexible and modular. Additional cooling units can be added together with rack fit-outs. This avoids the guesswork that accompanies room-based cooling.

Rack Cooling

In this approach, cooling is provided on a rack-by-rack basis. Specific air-conditioning units are dedicated to specific racks. This approach allows for maximum densities to be deployed per rack. However, this advantage can only be realized in data centers with fully loaded racks, otherwise, there would be too much cooling capacity, and air-conditioning losses alone can exceed the total IT load.

The rack-based cooling architecture is the most flexible and speedy to implement the solution. It achieves extreme density, but additional expenses may need to be incurred for effectiveness.

There is no best method – the cooling approach should depend on the peculiarities of the data center. It is desirable to combine different approaches in one data center for the highest cooling efficiency. However, we find that design trends favor the row-based approach. This is probably the safest option.

Cooling Path Elements

In the previous chapter, we discussed the different approaches to cooling and the components used to generate cooling. These components are collectively called capacity components. These include the CRAC/CRAH, Chillers, Cooling Towers, etc.

Heat naturally finds its way to a cooler region. However, to help it along the way and to channel it along a path, path elements are utilized. Some of these path elements include Pumps, Pipes, and Isolators.

Pump

A pump is a mechanical device used to move fluids in a particular direction. Pumps take in energy from a variety of sources and utilize the energy to perform the mechanical action used to move the fluid. Energy sources include manual operation, electricity, wind power, etc.

COOLING DISTRIBUTION

Pump (Source: Ruhrpumpen)

We know that due to gravitational force pull, there is an extant pressure in the earth's atmosphere. This is known as atmospheric pressure. However, this pressure might not be sufficient to move the fluid at a desirable flow rate. The objective of the pump is to overcome the operating pressure of the system so the fluid moves at the required rate of flow. The operating pressure is the pressure at different points of the fluid flow path which is a function of the elements along the path, the path cross-sectional area, the path length, elevation, obstructions, etc. The pump applies enough pressure to overwhelm inhibiting factors and move the fluid at the desired flow rate.

Pipe

A pipe is a tubular section or hollow cylinder, usually but not necessarily of circular cross-section, used mainly to convey flowing substances — liquids and gases (fluids), slurries, powders, and masses of small solids.

Copper Pipes (Source: Solitaire Overseas)

The cross-sectional area of the pipe and its orientation also affects the flow rate of the fluid.

A pipe can be made out of many types of material including ceramic, glass, fiberglass, many metals, concrete, and plastic. In refrigerant lines, aluminum pipes are mostly used. This is because other forms of metal may be incompatible with the service fluid or may be too heavy, and may retain some of the heat that needs to be transferred. In water lines, copper pipes are mostly used. However, for large water systems, steel pipes are used. This allows for a variety of pressure, temperature, and sizing requirements to meet the demands of chilled water systems.

Care should be taken to prevent corrosion in the pipe material. Protective layers are made around the racks to

COOLING DISTRIBUTION

prevent corrosion from the fluid action or underground soil action. Corrosion can cause leaks in the pipe or build up obstructions, both of which reduce the flow rate of the fluid.

The pipework could run above or below ground and at different orientations. All these must be taken into consideration when designing the piping system.

Isolators and Fittings

In pipes, fittings are attached to the line to dictate the direction of flow of the fluid. Examples of fittings are flanges and unions.

Isolators are used to resist the flow of a fluid along a pipe or other path. Examples of isolators are Isolation valves, shutoff valves, by-pass circuits, flanges and unions.

Isolators are used to prevent fluid flow downstream so as to allow for repair, replacement, maintenance, or upgrade of cooling capacity components and other cooling path elements. The isolators need to be properly sized so as to withstand the type fluid pressure, the fluid temperature, and the fluid type.

CHAPTER FOUR

DETERMINING THE NEED

The Concept of N

In many data center conversations, the concept of 'N' is a recurring feature, so much so that it may bring some confusion.

The N concept in data center parlance simply means Need. As the data center comprises of multifaceted fields of expertise, usage of the term "N" depends on the particular context. In the cooling system, "N" can be used in the context of **capacity**, or in the context of **quantity**.

In the context of capacity, "N" implies the total cooling capacity that needs to be available to keep the temperature in the room at an agreeable level. All the elements along the path to the load need to be sized accordingly as well.

The data center designer needs to determine N for cooling tower capacity, N for chiller capacity, N for CRAC/CRAH capacity, N for pump capacity, N for pipe sizes, N for valve sizes, and N for every other capacity component and path element that needs to operate for the data center to fulfill its objective effectively.

In the context of quantity, "N" implies the number of capacity components that need to be combined to provide the capacity required to cool the data center loads.

DETERMINING THE NEED

Suppose a Data Center is to be constructed to host a total of 60 racks. The operators wish to load an average capacity of 4kW on each rack, so that heat discharge would be at 4kW for every rack. Heat from other contributing sources is estimated to amount to 50kW. Therefore, the total capacity required for cooling the data hall would be 290kW. In the context of the data hall capacity, N = 290kW.

If we assume the cooling system employed is the air-cooled direct expansion system. If the cooling units procured by the operators each have a sensible cooling capacity of 30kW, they would require eight units to achieve the required cooling capacity. In this case, in the context of cooling unit quantities, N = 10.

As is seen from the above scenario, N could refer to any number of things. Therefore, when conceptualizing "N", one needs to clearly specify what context it is to be used.

Calculating N

The starting point of every data center design endeavor is to determine N, in the context capacity, required to deliver the business objectives.

Sizing the cooling system for a data center requires an understanding of the sources of heat to the critical spaces, the airflow distribution in the space, and the losses that may accrue from distributing cooling to these spaces. A needs assessment is carried out to ascertain these requirements.

Heat Sources

Heat sources to the room include electrical equipment, people, and the adjacent environment.

Electrical Equipment

All equipment that utilize electrical power to perform its operations generate heat. Essentially, all the power consumed by the equipment is converted to heat, since energy cannot be created or destroyed, but converted from one form to another. Therefore, the thermal output from electrical equipment in Watts simply equals its power input in Watts.

Electrical equipment include IT equipment, UPS, power distribution, air conditioning units, and lighting.

People

The body heat from people working in the data center hall also contributes to the thermal output in the room. It is estimated that the average human male gives up to 100 – 120 Watts of heat energy.

Environment and adjacent spaces

Ambient heat from the environment can seep through the room barriers, the walls, and the ceiling, into the critical area. The amount of heat absorbed depends on the heat conductivity of the materials used to demarcate the critical area.

If the rooms adjacent to the data center hall are at a higher temperature, heat could also enter the hall from these rooms. The adjacent rooms could be above, below, or beside the data center hall.

The heat gains from these adjacent environments can be derived if the U-value of the data center hall partitions are known.

The heat seeping through an external surface from the environment into the room can be computed with the following equation:

$$Q = U \times A \times \Delta T$$

Where

Q = Heat gained, in Watts (W)

U = Thermal transmittance (U-value) of the surface, in W/m²K

A = Total surface area, in square meters (m²)

ΔT = Difference in temperature between the room and the ambient environment, in Kelvin (K)

As what is considered in the data center is net-sensible heat, the temperature here refers to the dry-bulb temperature.

Consider a hypothetical situation where the data center hall is partitioned on all six sides (ceiling above, floor below, right side, left side, front side, and backside) with the cavity wall discussed in Chapter One. Suppose also that each of these sides has a total surface area of 100m² and the dry-bulb temperature outside the room on all sides is 39°C. If we intend to keep the dry-bulb temperature in the data center hall at 23°C, what would be the total heat gains into the hall from the external environment?

Recall that this cavity wall has a thermal transmittance (U-value) of 0.61 W/m²K. Therefore, from each side, the heat gained is:

$$Q = U \times A \times \Delta T$$
$$= 0.61 \times 100 \times 16$$
$$= 976W$$

As the data center is expected to last for up to 20 years before any major upgrade or rework is done, the Uptime Institute recommends that cooling should be designed for extreme temperatures over a 20 year period. The American Society of Heating, Refrigerating and Air-Conditioning Engineers (ASHRAE) has collated and maintains climate data for all regions across the world. The resources can be accessed on their website here:

https://www.ashrae.org/technical-resources/bookstore/weather-data-center

While it is possible to perform a complete enumeration of all heat contributors and compute the heat removal requirements, a quick estimate of the data center cooling capacity requirements can be estimated with relative accuracy using some simple rules. These rules have been arrived at by observing relationships in many data centers. However, it must be noted that some margin of error should be allowed as this estimation may not give the same value as a more detailed analysis.

S/N	Item	Data required	Heat output (W)
1	IT equipment	Total IT load power in Watts	Same as total IT load power in watts
2	UPS with battery	Power system rated power in Watts	(0.04 x Power system rating) + (0.05 x Total IT load power)
3	Power distribution	Power system rated power in Watts	(0.01 x Power system rating) + (0.02 x Total IT load power)
4	Lighting	Floor area in square feet, or Floor area in square meters	2.0 x floor area (sq ft), or 21.53 x floor area (sq m)
5	People	Max no of personnel in data center	100 x Max no of personnel
6	Heat gains from environment		1.1 x (sum of #1 to #5)
	Total	**Subtotals from above**	**Sum of heat output subtotals**

Cooling Requirement Estimation

DETERMINING THE NEED

When selecting a cooling unit to deploy, it is important to pick one that gives the desired capacity given the design conditions. The net sensible cooling capacity from the unit will vary depending on the presented conditions. Some of these conditions include elevation with respect to sea level, the outside air temperature, the type of refrigerant used, the return air temperature, and the desired supply air temperature.

The closer the supply temperature is to the return temperature, the faster it takes to bring the room to the desired temperature. This reduces the length of time the unit operates thus saving power.

The cooling unit manufacturers typically detail the unit's performance specifications at given design conditions. Consider the screenshot below:

	CRO35RA				
Unit inlet air temperature	37.0	°C	Sea level	41	m
Unit inlet air relative humidity	50.0	%	Refrigerant	R410A	
Unit airflow	5545	m³/h	Unit power supply	400 V/3 ph/50 Hz	
Outdoor air temperature	41.0	°C	Compressor modulation	100	%
			Unit performances		
Unit	CRO35RA		Unit power input	9.67	kW
Gross total cooling capacity	37.9	kW	Net total cooling capacity	36.8	kW
Gross sensible cooling capacity	37.9	kW	Net sensible cooling capacity	36.8	kW
SHR	1.00		Unit EER	3.81	
Off coil air temperature	16.4	°C	Internal filter class (EN779 std)	G4	
Off coil air relative humidity	80.5	%	Width	600	mm
Room SPL (@ 2m, f.f)	70.0	dB(A)	Depth	1175	mm
Condensing temperature	45.0	°C	Height	2000	mm
Supply air temperature	16.4	°C	Weight	365	kg

These are the performance specifications of a Vertiv DX cooling unit. If hot air returns to the unit at 37°C and cold air is supplied at 16.4°C, the net sensible cooling capacity is 36.8kW at the given environmental conditions and refrigerant type. The air supply flow rate is given as 5545m³/h.

The screenshot below represents performance specifications for a Schneider Electric chilled water CRAH.

Performance specifications 12.7°C (55°F) EWT (ACRC600/ACRC600P series)

Temperature DB, WB – °C (°F)	CW Delta T – °C (°F)	Total Net Capacity – kW (BTU/hr)	Sensible Net Capacity – kW (BTU/hr)	Sensible Heat Ratio – SHR	CW Flow Rate – l/s (GPM)	Total CW Pressure Drop – kPa (ft H2O)
26.7°C DB, 17.1°C WB (80°F DB, 62.8°F WB)						
	5.5°C (10°F)	24.7 (85000)	24.7 (85000)	1.00	1.2 (18.3)	33 (11.3)
	6.6°C (12°F)	22.3 (76000)	22.3 (76000)	1.00	0.9 (13.9)	20 (6.7)
	7.7°C (14°F)	20.0 (68000)	20.0 (68000)	1.00	0.7 (10.8)	12 (4.2)
	8.8°C (16°F)	17.8 (61000)	17.8 (61000)	1.00	0.5 (8.6)	8 (2.8)
	10.0°C (18°F)	15.8 (54000)	15.8 (54000)	1.00	0.4 (6.9)	5 (1.8)
	11.1°C (20°F)	13.9 (48000)	13.9 (48000)	1.00	0.4 (5.6)	4 (1.2)
29.4°C DB, 18.1°C WB (85°F DB, 64.5°F WB)						
	5.5°C (10°F)	31.3 (107000)	31.3 (107000)	1.00	1.4 (22.6)	50 (16.9)
	6.6°C (12°F)	28.5 (97000)	28.5 (97000)	1.00	1.1 (17.3)	30 (10.2)
	7.7°C (14°F)	25.8 (88000)	25.8 (88000)	1.00	0.9 (13.6)	19 (6.5)
	8.8°C (16°F)	23.3 (80000)	23.3 (80000)	1.00	0.7 (10.8)	8 (4.2)
	10.0°C (18°F)	21.0 (72000)	21.0 (72000)	1.00	0.6 (8.8)	8 (2.8)
	11.1°C (20°F)	18.7 (64000)	18.7 (64000)	1.00	0.5 (7.2)	6 (1.8)
32.2°C DB, 18.9°C WB (90°F DB, 66.1°F WB)						
	5.5°C (10°F)	39.1 (133000)	39.1 (133000)	1.00	1.7 (27.7)	75 (24.9)
	6.6°C (12°F)	35.9 (123000)	35.9 (123000)	1.00	1.3 (21.3)	45 (15.02)
	7.7°C (14°F)	32.8 (112000)	32.8 (112000)	1.00	1.1 (16.9)	20 (9.7)
	8.8°C (16°F)	30.0 (102000)	30.0 (102000)	1.00	0.9 (13.6)	19 (6.5)
	10.0°C (18°F)	27.2 (93000)	27.2 (93000)	1.00	0.7 (11.1)	13 (4.4)
35.0°C DB, 19.8°C WB (95°F DB, 67.7°F WB)						
	6.6°C (12°F)	44.2 (151000)	44.2 (151000)	1.00	1.6 (25.9)	66 (21.9)
	7.7°C (14°F)	40.8 (139000)	40.8 (139000)	1.00	1.3 (20.6)	42 (14.1)
	8.8°C (16°F)	37.5 (128000)	37.5 (128000)	1.00	1.1 (16.7)	28 (9.5)

DETERMINING THE NEED

If cold water arrives from the chiller at 12.7°C and returns at 19.3°C[3], and hot air from the room is taken in at 32.2°C, the net sensible cooling capacity is 35.9kW. The chilled water flow rate at this point is given as 1.3 liters/sec.

We can observe that the closer the temperature difference between the chiller cold water supply and hot water return, the higher the unit cooling capacity.

Air Flow

Recall that heat flows from a region of higher temperature to that of lower temperature. Also, when the heat is absorbed, the object's temperature rises.

Consider an equipment rack populated with IT devices that together consume a total electrical power of 5kW, all of which will be converted into heat. Now, when air flows through the IT devices, the 5kW of heat gets transferred to the air, so that the air becomes hotter when it is discharged from the IT devices.

Assume that the air entering the rack has a temperature of 23°C. Twenty seconds later, we see all that air at the back of the rack, but now at a temperature of 34°C. How does this come about?

---

[3] the temperature difference ΔT between cold and hot water is 6.6°C

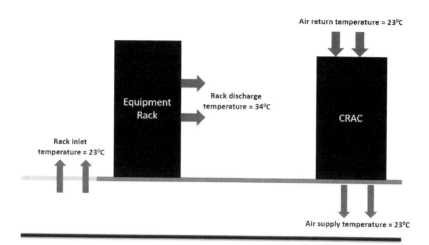

The temperature that the air rises to depends on the volume of the air that passes through the IT devices at a time. Therefore, to maintain a minimum rack inlet temperature air and a maximum rack discharge temperature, we need to ensure an appropriate airflow rate. How can we determine this?

Remember the heat transfer equation?

$$Q = mc\Delta T$$

In our scenario, the object that rises in temperature is air.

Q, which is the heat transferred, is 5kW

c, which is the specific heat capacity of air at constant pressure, is 1kJ/kg/°C

ΔT, which is the change in air temperature, 11°C

Therefore, to achieve the temperature rise, the total mass of the air flowing is:

$$m = \frac{Q}{c\Delta T}$$

$$= \frac{5}{1 \times 11}$$

$$= 0.46 kg$$

Recall also that the density of an object is its mass divided by its volume.

$$density = \frac{mass}{volume}$$

The density of air is 1.2 kg/m³. Therefore, air weighing 0.46kg will have a volume of:

$$volume = \frac{mass}{density}$$

$$= \frac{0.46}{1.2}$$

$$= 0.38 m^3$$

Now, it took 20 seconds to record the rise in temperature. Recall that:

$$flow\ rate = \frac{volume}{time}$$

So that the air flows at a rate of:

$$= \frac{0.38}{20} m^3/s$$

$$= 0.019 m^3/s$$

Therefore, for air to absorb a sensible heat of 5kW and have only an 11°C rise in temperature in 20 seconds, it must maintain a flow rate of 0.38m³/s.

In our scenario, the cold air reaches the racks through the openings in the perforated tile. What must be the

DETERMINING THE NEED

aggregate cross-sectional area of the tile openings to maintain the flow rate?

Recall again that flow rate can also be calculated as follows:

$$\textit{Flow Rate} = \textit{Cross-sectional Area} \times \textit{Velocity of Flow}$$

Assume that the cooling unit discharges the cold air at a velocity constant velocity of 0.19m/s. It follows that the perforated tile must have a minimum aggregate cross-sectional of:

$$\textit{Cross-sectional Area} = \frac{\textit{Flow Rate}}{\textit{Velocity of Flow}}$$
$$= \frac{0.019}{0.19}$$
$$= 0.1 m^2$$

The above is a simple scenario that assumes a 100% heat exchange between the IT equipment components and the flowing air. In reality, some of the heat will be trapped on the body of the equipment, inside the rack, or someplace else.

Also, it is unlikely that all of the air leaving the perforated tiles will find its way into the rack. Some of it may drift sideways to other places. Modern installations try to curtail this by enclosing the cold-aisle so that the air is contained. This will ensure that all the cold air is available to the IT racks.

In addition, estimating the airflow velocity is complicated. It is highly unlikely that the discharge speed with which the air leaves the cooling unit will be the speed at which the air passes through the perforated tiles. An accurate measurement may require a CFD analysis. A better approach is to have the cooling units installed in-row with the IT racks. This will minimize travel time of the cold air from the cooling units to the rack.

It is common place nowadays to find in-row cooling units utilized in tandem with hot-aisle or cold-aisle containments. However, during design calculations, it is good practice to integrate a safety factor of 5 – 10% to cover for possible losses.

Refrigerant Lines

Recall that typically, the cooling unit removes heat from the room via the refrigeration cycle. The refrigerant absorbs the heat from the hot air entering the unit and takes it outside the room, going through a number of processes and changes along the way.

DETERMINING THE NEED

The refrigerant is a cold gas at the beginning of the cycle. It becomes a liquid during the cycle and returns to its original form at the end of the cycle. The piping through which the refrigerant flows as a gas is called the *Suction Line* while that through which it flows a liquid is called the *Liquid Line*.

Computing the diameter of the suction and liquid lines is quite complicated. There are different types of refrigerant gas in use for commercial applications, each with differing heat capacities. In addition, as the refrigerant is compresses and expands, its flow rate will fluctuate. Finally, the site topology may warrant bends, turns, and elevations. All of these must be factored in the design.

Luckily, cooling unit manufacturers generally specify guidelines for refrigerant piping. The data center designer should clarify the design requirements to competent HVAC engineers and work with them to achieve the desired outcomes.

Water Lines

Water is an incompressible fluid. Therefore, it maintains the same volume at all times when flowing through a medium. This makes designing the piping much easier than that of refrigeration lines. Simply, the flow rate required to maintain the desired room temperature will determine the pipe cross-sectional area and velocity of flow.

ASHRAE specifies velocity limits for chilled water pipes in its handbook (https://www.ashrae.org/technical-resources/ashrae-handbook). It also specifies pressure drop limits for various pipe sizes running over specific distances. For instances, for pipes with a 2 inch or smaller diameter, the velocity limit is 1.2m/s, and the pressure drop limit is 1m for every 25m of pipe.

Therefore, when we have a target flow rate, we select the pipe material and cross-sectional area that will allow the flow rate given the velocity limitations specified by the standards. Most pipe manufacturers will state the maximum velocity limits of the different types and sizes of pipes that they make.

Consider the schematic below:

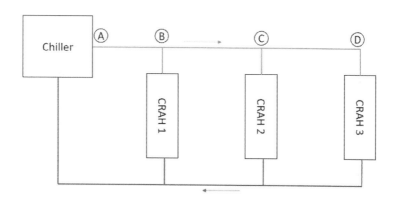

Chilled Water System Schematic

DETERMINING THE NEED

This is a closed-loop system with cold water leaving the chiller to return as hot water. If we assume that CRAH 1, CRAH 2, and CRAH 3 each require a flow rate of $10m^3/s$, the Chiller would need to discharge water at a minimum flow rate of $30m^3/s$.

	Flow Rate (m^3/s)
CRAH 1	10
CRAH 2	10
CRAH 3	10
Chiller	30

At point A, the pipe would be sized to allow a flow rate of $30m^3/s$. On reaching point B, some of the water veers off to CRAH 1. Therefore, the pipe to CRAH 1 will be sized for a flow rate of $10m^3/s$, while the pipe heading to point C is sized for a flow rate of $20m^3/s$.

At point C, a similar thing happens, some of the water veers off to CRAH 2. The pipe to CRAH 2 will be sized for a flow rate of $10m^3/s$, while the pipe heading to point C is sized for a flow rate of $10m^3/s$.

At point D, the pipe bends and enters into CRAH 3.

	Flow Rate (m³/s)
Point A to Point B	30
Point B to Point C	20
Point C to Point D	10
Point B to CRAH 1	10
Point C to CRAH 2	10
Point D to CRAH 3	10

Appropriate pipe fittings are used to attach wider pipes to narrower pipes.

In real situations, other factors that may introduce more complexities need to be considered. As water travels through the line, its pressure drops so that the flow rate is impacted. Likewise, pipe fittings, pipe lengths, gravity, contours, and even the equipment cause pressure drops. Therefore, secondary pumps may need to be introduced to shore up the flow rate.

Many mechanical design tools automate material selection based on design specifications and attendant constraints. The data center designer should clarify the design requirements to competent HVAC engineers and work with them to achieve the desired outcomes given the foundational knowledge s/he now possesses.

Redundancy

Several redundancy expressions exist in literature. The most common examples are N + 1, 2N, and 2(N+1). These expressions refer to N in the context of quantities needed to deliver required capacities.

N + 1 describes a system with N quantities of capacity components, and an extra component with the same capacity as those providing the N capacity.

2N describes a situation where there are two separate systems, System A and System B, each providing N capacity from N components.

2(N + 1) describes a situation where there are two separate systems, System A and System B, each consisting of N + 1 capacity components.

Tier Specification

Originally defined by the Uptime Institute, the tier specification classifies data centers with regard to their complexity and in-built redundancies.

There are four data center tiers.

Tier I – Basic Capacity

A data center designed for Tier I only has the basic required capacity components and path elements, without any redundancy.

Any planned or unplanned disruptions for maintenance, repairs, or upgrades will necessitate the complete shutdown of the data center until the activity is completed.

Tier I data centers have an expected uptime of 99.671% (28.8 hours of downtime annually).

Tier II – Redundant Capacity

A data center designed for Tier II only has redundancy in all the capacity components. However, there is no redundancy in the heat removal path. Only the basic required path elements are present.

Any planned activity on the capacity components may not require a shutdown of the entire facility. However, unplanned disruptions will result in a shutdown. Planned or unplanned interruptions to path elements will shut down the facility.

Tier II data centers have an expected uptime of 99.741% (22 hours of downtime annually).

Tier III – Concurrently Maintainable

A data center designed for Tier III has redundancy in all the capacity components. It also has redundant paths through which cooling can get to the critical equipment. All the redundant paths do not need to be active at the same time.

Any planned activity on the capacity components does not require a shutdown of the entire facility. Likewise, works on any path element do not necessitate an outage. Cooling can simply be provided through other paths. Unplanned activities however may result in an outage.

A Tier III data center with proper operational processes can function without shutting down throughout its lifetime.

Tier III data centers have an expected uptime of 99.982% (1.6 hours of downtime annually).

Tier IV – Fault Tolerant

Like the Tier III data center, a Tier IV data center also has redundancy in capacity components and path elements, with at least two cooling paths always active.

The complementary capacity components and cooling paths are physically compartmentalized from each other. Planned and unplanned interruptions will not hamper the data center operation. There is an autonomous response to failure.

Tier III data centers have an expected uptime of 99.995% (26.3 minutes of downtime annually).

The decision on which tier specification goal to aim for depends on the business needs. The business must weigh its design goals against the investment implications.

A data center with applications running tasks that can be managed manually for a short period without any significant impact on revenue can make do with a Tier I data center. To reduce the possible downtime period, the business can invest in redundancies to some components, like the CRAH, or fully upscale to Tier II.

Most data center owners have found that aiming for a Tier III rating has an economically efficient reliability outcome when compared to Tier IV data centers, which are significantly more expensive to operate, as all the capacity components need to work concurrently.

Installing standard operational procedures and a rigorous maintenance regime in a Tier III data center can prevent unplanned outages of which Tier IV data centers are tolerant, at a lower cost.

However, for applications that are highly intolerant any sort of outage, investing in a Tier IV data center might make more economic sense as against the incurred revenue losses that the outage would cause.

CHAPTER FIVE
COOLING EFFICIENCY

The Need for Efficiency

As more and more services get offered and consumed digitally, more and more IT equipment are deployed.

As more and more IT equipment are deployed, more and more data centers are commissioned.

As more and more data centers are commissioned, more and more cooling is needed.

As more and more cooling is needed, more and more electrical energy is generated and used.

As more and more electrical energy is used, there is more and more reason for us to worry as a race. We are continuously altering our ecological landscape. The fact that data centers have to run 24 x 365 hours in a year certainly does not help.

The worry stems from the *how* through which electrical energy is generated, and the *what* that happens to the electrical energy after is used.

Energy cannot be created or destroyed, only transformed. Electrical energy is generated through the transformation from other sources. And after usage by IT equipment, it is transformed into another form.

The most common energy form from which electrical energy is generated is through chemical energy stored in fossil fuels. The actual mechanism is out of our scope, but it suffices to say that the fuels are burned. The burning releases energy in the form of heat before other eventual transformations to electricity.

Some of the heat generated is lost to the environment. In addition, some gases are emitted to the atmosphere, most of which are bad for the environment, especially the carbon brothers, Carbon Dioxide (CO_2) and Carbon Monoxide (CO). CO eventually becomes CO_2 anyway, after exposure to Oxygen in the atmosphere.

When cooling is provided to the IT equipment, the electrical energy consumed is transformed to heat energy. Which is also emitted to the environment.

The heat energies for generation and usage, coupled with the release of so-called greenhouse gases (chiefly CO_2) to the earth's atmosphere, have the collective effect of changing the earth's natural atmospheric circumstances, a phenomenon known as Global Warming[4]. There is ample literature on the likely effects of global warming. In summary, it is **not** good.

This grim reality will certainly not shut down data centers. It behooves us, data center designers, to find

---

[4] Climate Change, also called Global Warming, refers to the rise in average surface temperatures on Earth.

COOLING EFFICIENCY

creative and efficient ways of generating, and minimizing, usage of energy in our data centers.

The Data Center is not the only building that uses energy, some would argue. Why must it the prerogative of designers to prioritize energy efficiency? Well, for starters, a typical enterprise data center may consume as much as 40 times as much energy a similarly sized office would consume.

Beyond altruism, worrying about energy efficiency has a significant impact on the bottom-line. Energy costs continue to rise, especially against the backdrop of the unstable political landscape. Industry regulators have also started to apply pressure to enforce environmental restrictions.

Data Center Cooling System designers need to explore ways to reduce the cooling units deployed to the barest minimum.

Industry surveys carried out around 2017 revealed that data centers account for up to 3% of global electricity usage. That number is closer to 5% today, and these numbers will keep increasing.

The data center stakeholders must place cooling and energy efficiency front, back, and center. And that starts with saving as much energy as possible.

Cooling Efficiency Metrics

It is common knowledge in management circles that if you want real growth and results, you need to measure what matters. *What matters* are the indicators, key metrics that show whether you are achieving your objectives, and if not, how far off the objectives you are.

Our objective is to ensure as much cooling efficiency as possible. We want to make sure we deploy only as much as we need. And we want as much as possible to minimize what we need.

How do we know if we are achieving our objectives or not? Whether to pat ourselves at the back or return to the drawing board? Whether to double down on what we are doing or step backward? We know through cooling efficiency indicators.

The data center industry has agreed upon some metrics to measure data center cooling performance. Among these are the following:

Rack Cooling Index (RCI)®

Originally designed and published by ANCIS Incorporated[5], the Rack Cooling Index (RCI)® has now been adopted by industry authorities, including ASHRAE,

---

[5] www.ancis.us

ANSI/BICSI, and The Green Grid. It has also been referenced by the U.S. Department of Energy.

The Rack Cooling Index (RCI)® is a measure of how effectively racks are cooled and kept within industry thermal guidelines and standards. The ASHRAE guidelines state that IT equipment intake air should be kept within the range of 18°C and 27°C[6]. Beyond the lower limit, the air is overcooled and tremendous savings can be made. Beyond the upper limit, the air is undercooled and there is a risk of damage to IT equipment.

The RCI® helps operators maintain a balance between cooling sufficiency and the cost of cooling.

The RCI metric compresses the intake temperatures (measured or modeled) into two numbers: RCI(HI) and RCI(LO). Both are expressed as a percentage with maximum values of 100%.

An RCI(HI) of 100% indicates that there are no intake temperatures above the maximum recommended. The further the value goes below 100%, the higher the risk of equipment exposure to temperatures above the maximum recommended limits.

An RCI(LO) of 100% indicates that there are no intake temperatures above the minimum recommended. The

---

[6] ASHRAE regularly reviews its design guidelines. Visit the ASHRAE website for the latest design specifications.

further the value goes below 100%, the higher the risk of costs wasted to overcooling.

A data center with absolute compliance to industry standards will have both RCI(HI) and RCI(LO) at 100%. RCI can be computed at the rack level, at the row level, and at the data center level.

It is important to note that even if supply temperatures from the cooling unit is within recommended guidelines, the actual air intake into the rack might not be. Optimizing RCI values might require increasing or decreasing the volume of supply air, slightly increasing or reducing the supply air temperature, increasing or reducing air flow-rate, shifting the positioning of IT equipment, installing additional perforated tiles, ducting of supply air, or changing the positioning of the cooling equipment.

To compute the RCI, data is polled numerous times from adequately installed sensors or through a CFD analysis. This is now fed into the RCI formula as follows:

$$RCI(HI) = \left(1 - \frac{Total\ Overtemperature}{Maximum\ Allowable\ Overtemperature}\right) \times 100\%$$

$$= \left(1 - \frac{\Sigma(T_x - T_{max-rec})_{T_x > T_{max-rec}}}{n \times (T_{max-all} - T_{max-rec})}\right) \times 100\%$$

COOLING EFFICIENCY

Where

T_x = Measured temperature intake at a point x in time

n = number of times data was polled

$T_{max-rec}$ = Maximum recommended temperature according to ASHRAE or other industry standard

$T_{max-all}$ = Maximum allowable temperature before equipment gets damaged

It should be noted that

$$T_x - T_{max-rec}$$

cannot be less than zero. Every point where the polled temperature is less than the maximum recommended value is discarded.

Likewise,

$$RCI(LO) = \left(1 - \frac{Total\ Undertemperature}{Maximum\ Allowable\ Undertemperature}\right) \times 100\%$$

$$= \left(1 - \frac{\sum (T_{min-rec} - T_x)_{T_x < T_{min-rec}}}{n \times (T_{min-rec} - T_{min-all})}\right) \times 100\%$$

Where

> T_x = Measured temperature intake at a point x in time
>
> n = number of times data was polled
>
> $T_{min\text{-}rec}$ = Minimum recommended temperature according to ASHRAE or other industry standard
>
> $T_{min\text{-}all}$ = Minimum allowable temperature before equipment gets damaged

It should be noted that

$$T_{min\text{-}rec} - T_x$$

cannot be less than zero. Every point where the polled temperature is greater than the minimum recommended value is discarded.

An ASHRAE paper discussing the RCI in some detail can be seen here:

http://www.ancis.us/images/RCI--for_Website.pdf

The document describes the RCI for analyzing, reporting, and specifying the thermal environment in data centers, telecom central offices, and other mission critical facilities.

Return Temperature Index (RTI)™

Like the RCI®, the RCI™ was designed and published by ANCIS Incorporated[7]. The index has also now been adopted by industry authorities, including ASHRAE, ANSI/BICSI, and The Green Grid. It has also been referenced by the U.S. Department of Energy.

The Return Temperature Index (RTI)™ is a measure of the energy efficiency and performance of the equipment room air-management system, expressed as a percentage.

Two common air-circulations problems plague the data center. These are by-pass air and recirculated air. *By-pass air* is cold air that is returned to the cooling unit without being passed through the IT equipment that need cooling. This results in wasted energy. *Recirculated air* is hot air that is repeatedly passed through IT equipment without being cooled. This can cause damage to the IT equipment.

RTI ™ helps detect and address these problems. An RTI value of less than 100% indicates the presence of by-pass air. An RTI value of greater than 100% indicates the presence of recirculated air. When RTI is at 100%, the cooling performance is said to be efficient.

$$RTI = \left(\frac{T_{return} - T_{supply}}{\Delta T_{equipment}}\right) \times 100\%$$

---

[7] www.ancis.us

Where,

T_{return} = Average return air temperature

T_{supply} = Average supply air temperature

$\Delta T_{equipment}$ = Temperature rise across the IT equipment

Rating	RTI
Optimal	100%
Bypass	<100%
Recirculation	>100%

A combination of the RCI and RTI metrics provides comprehensive insights into the cooling performance and the cost penalty of trying to enforce absolute performance. Achieving an RCI value of 100% usually requires lowering the supply pressure or increasing the air flow-rate, both of which come at an energy cost. The RTI helps quantity how much this cost is.

An ASHRAE paper discussing the RTI in some detail can be seen here:

http://www.ancis.us/images/SL-08-018_Final.pdf

The document also demonstrates the usage of the RTI in combination with the RCI.

Performance Indicator (PI)

In 2007, The Green Grid, a consortium of participants from different facets of the data center ecosystem dedicated to improving data center efficiency, published the PUE metric. This metric has found much acceptance in the data center industry. The Green Grid's Performance Indicator (PI) builds on the PUE[8].

The Performance Indicator (PI) is a set of metrics that access a data center's power and cooling effectiveness. These metrics are the PUE ratio (PUEr), IT Thermal Conformance, and IT Thermal Resilience.

PUE Ratio (PUEr)

The PUE ratio assesses the energy efficiency of a data center as a percentage. It expresses how far away a data center is from its target PUE range. The PUEr is calculated as follows:

---

[8] We discussed the PUE in detail in the book "Designing Data Centers - Book 1: Power" available on Amazon.

$$PUEr = \left(\frac{Target\ PUE}{Current\ PUE}\right) \times 100\%$$

Assume a data center targets a PUE of 1.35 but is currently has a PUE of 1.5. The PUEr would be:

$$PUEr = \left(\frac{1.35}{1.5}\right) \times 100\% = 90\%$$

IT Thermal Conformance

IT Thermal Conformance measures the efficiency of a data center's cooling system. It assesses how efficiently equipment is cooled during normal IT operations.

IT Thermal Conformance is the proportion of IT equipment operating within the ASHRAE recommended ranges. It is calculated as follows:

$IT\ Thermal\ Conformance =$

$\left(\frac{IT\ Equipment\ within\ ASHRAE\ recommended\ ranges}{Total\ number\ of\ IT\ Equipment}\right) \times 100\%$

IT Thermal Resilience

IT Thermal Resilience measures the resilience of a data center's cooling system. It is the IT Thermal Conformance when all redundant cooling systems are turned off, possibly for maintenance, repair, or replacement. It measures the likelihood of an outage when redundant capacity components are removed.

It is calculated the same way as the IT Thermal Conformance, except that the collation of equipment operating within ASHRAE recommended ranges is done when redundant cooling units are turned off.

The Performance Indicator (PI) combines these three metrics to give a wholesome view of the status of the data center's efficiency, performance, and resilience. The PI recognizes that these three characteristics are linked so that a change in one can affect the other two. Raising the operating temperature for instance will improve efficiency, but might affect performance. Increasing efficiency might also result in sacrificing resilience.

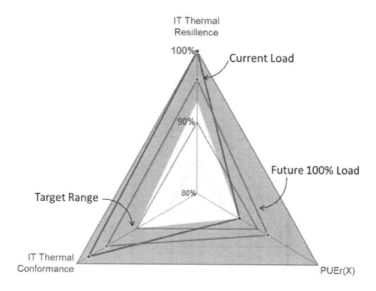

Performance Indicator Visualization
(Source: The Green Grid)

Modelling software can be used to simulate varying values of these three characteristics to allow operators predict the effect of changes made to the data center.

There are four levels of PI assessment depending on the amount of data collected.

Level 1: Data is collected at the rack level. Temperature sensors are installed at the top, middle, and bottom of every rack in line with ASHRAE recommendations.

Level 2: Data is collected at the server level. Each server is instrumented with a temperature monitoring component.

Level 3: Data is collected at the rack level similar to Level 1. However, this data is used to create a model that can be used to simulate future scenarios.

Level 4: Data is collected from every point in the data center – the racks, the servers, the floors, the cooling unit supply, and return, etc. The data is used to create a much more accurate model for future simulations.

Water Usage Effectiveness (WUE)

Water Usage Effectiveness is a member of the family of xUE efficiency metrics developed by The Green Grid. Other prominent members of the family are Power Usage Effectiveness (PUE) and Carbon Usage Effectiveness (CUE). Used together, these metrics provide a holistic view of the energy and environmental efficiency of the data center.

The Water Usage Efficiency (WUE) of a data center is a value that shows how much of the water is used by the data center to keep its operations running. With many data centers adopting energy-saving approaches to cooling like evaporative cooling, cooling towers, etc, water is increasingly becoming more important to the data center. However, diverting clean water from other critical uses, such as drinking and cooking, does have its negative effects. It is important to limit water use to the barest minimum vis-à-vis the potential energy savings.

WUE helps to keep track of the data center's water use, helping to attain the objective of wanting to make sure we use only as much water as we need.

The WUE is calculated as follows:

$$WUE = \frac{Annual\ Water\ Usage}{Total\ energy\ used\ by\ IT\ equipment}$$

It has a unit of liters/kilowatt-hour (L/kWh).

The Green Grid defines water usage as *"the water use in processes due to site operations and source energy generation"*. Therefore, the WUE only considers water on site for the operation of the data center facility e.g. water used for cooling, for humidification, for power generation, etc.

The ideal value for the WUE is 0.0, meaning that no water is used in the facility. Minimal water use can be achieved by using only Direct Expansion (DX) systems. However, this will incur additional energy costs, potentially impacting the PUE and the CUE.

The Green Grid defines another variation of the WUE, the WUE_{source}.

$$WUE_{source} = \frac{Annual\ Source\ Energy\ Water\ Usage + Annual\ Water\ Usage}{Total\ energy\ used\ by\ IT\ equipment}$$

The WUE_{source} metric recognizes that some of the energy used in the data center is generated from sources external to the data center. The water used for generating this external energy is accounted for in the WUE_{source} metric.

It may then be argued that water is also used for manufacturing all the mechanical and electrical equipment used in the data center. Shouldn't these be part of the WUE metric? The Green Grid keeps updating its research work to define metrics that help measure water and energy efficiency in the data center. It suffices to say that as the data center market tends to efficient equipment, the supply chain of non-efficient equipment will be impacted thus slowly eliminating these equipment from data center facilities. Thus the concern of manufacturing costs for inefficient equipment will be indirectly dealt with.

Cooling Efficiency Best Practices

There are several opportunities to optimize the efficiency of the cooling system in the data center. Some of these include:

Aisle Arrangement

As described in an earlier section, data centers should arrange IT racks in a hot-aisle/cold-aisle arrangement following the 7-tile pitch rule.

To make the most of this arrangement, there needs to be appropriate ventilation in the equipment cabinet. The front, and back, of the cabinet need to be adequately perforated to allow a good flow of air through to the equipment.

Aisle Containment

An increasingly popular strategy, aisle containment involves the complete demarcation of the cold aisle or hot aisle, so that the cold air, or hot air, is contained in the aisle. This eliminates the inadvertent mixing of cold air with hot air, providing the maximum benefit of the 7-tile pitch arrangement.

It is generally less complex to contain the cold air so that the general environment in the data center becomes hotter while the inlet to the IT equipment becomes a lot colder. If hot air is to be contained, a mechanism to channel the hot air out to the cooling units needs to be installed.

This brings about another complexity. If we contain the cold air and allow hot air to discharge to the environment, how do we cool the room for the workers in the Data Center?

Manufacturers have reacted by designing cooling units to stand in line with the IT racks and cabinets, in the same row. Units like these are generally referred to as In-Row Units.

COOLING EFFICIENCY

With the use of In-Row units, the hot air can instead be contained. The In-Row units can then suck in the hot air as it is discharged from the IT equipment. More and more data center designers are favoring this approach.

Sealed Rooms

The data center should be completely sealed to prevent the escape of cold air to the external environment. This could progressively worsen the energy situation as more and more energy is consumed to adequately cool the server room space only for the cold air to escape to other areas.

Airflow Management

Open spaces in the cabinets should be minimized as much as possible. This can be done by placing blanking plates in unused rack unit spaces, blocking cabinet sides, and making use of perforated front and back doors.

Cable Management

Cables impede airflow in the data center. They must be properly managed and routed to enable cold air to reach its desired destination.

Equipment Inlet Temperature/Humidity Adjustments

We have seen that raising the supply temperature of the cooling unit reduces the energy needed to maintain the cooling system.

ASHRAE defines four classes of IT equipment. These are:

Class A1 - operating between 15°C and 32°C at 20% to 80% relative humidity

Class A2 - operating between 10°C and 35°C at 20% to 80% relative humidity

Class A3 - operating between 5°C and 40°C at 8% to 85% relative humidity

Class A4 - operating between 5°C and 45°C at 8% to 80% relative humidity

For all classes, the recommended temperature range is 18°C and 27°C.

Data center operators seldom set up their data centers to operate close to the upper limit of the ASHRAE guidelines. This is because it is known that any unplanned interruptions to the cooling system will result in a rapid rise in room temperature. If the normal operating temperature is relatively high, then this rapid temperature rise can cause immediate damage or outage to the IT equipment.

However, modern IT equipment will operate safely at temperature levels beyond the ASHRAE recommended ranges. For instance, most modern servers can run effectively at temperatures up to 32°C, with some manufacturers even specifying as high as 40°C. Raising the equipment inlet temperatures by 1 or 2 degrees will save energy and operational costs without any significant effect on the data center operations.

Variable Speed Fan Drives (VSD)

Cooling equipment fans can account for up to 10% of a data center's electrical load. Cooling equipment with fans that cannot vary their speeds will continue to operate at full capacity even when other cooling efficiency mechanisms like containment and hot-aisle/cold-aisle are employed. This problem is exacerbated when a data center has multiple cooling units for efficiency.

With VSDs, the cooling equipment can vary its operation as the electrical load varies, thus saving energy.

Air-Side and Water-Side Economizers

We have discussed how air-side and water-side economizers operate. All data centers in every climatic region can employ some sort of economization technique, partially and fully, to their cooling systems.

The above has been a discussion on cooling efficiency for the data center. Data center designers should endeavor to work with cooling experts to design highly energy-efficient data centers.

Next we will examine the codes and standards relevant to cooling in the data center.

CHAPTER SIX
CODES AND STANDARDS

To maintain a minimum standard for quality and safety, every country has supervisory bodies that set regulations, rules and codes defining electrical installations. Flouting these rules may have legal implications. Hence, the data center cooling system designer needs to be familiar with the applicable rules set by the Authorities Having Jurisdiction (AHJ) in their region.

In addition to the local AHJs, there are globally recognized bodies that set standards for data center design. These standards exist to streamline design practices so that all data centers complying with the standards can provide the same outcome, regardless of geographical location.

Some of the well-known standards bodies include the following:

Uptime Institute

The very first and most widely recognized standards body is the Uptime Institute, which came up with the Tier rating system in 1995. They meticulously define that the Tier rating system measures data center design outcomes, differing greatly from other standards, which detail specific checklists that must be followed.

Data Center designs are classified as either Tier I, Tier II, Tier III, or Tier IV, depending on design objectives and outcomes. The highest tier level does not necessarily indicate the best design, rather it is business objectives that determine the best tier level to target.

Details of the Uptime Institute Tier Classification can be seen here:

https://uptimeinstitute.com/tiers

TIA

The Telecommunications Industry Association (TIA) is a body renowned for network cabling standards. Its cabling standards cover Buildings, Campuses, and more recently, Data Centers.

The TIA, in conjunction with the American National Standards Institute (ANSI), created the TIA-942 Data Center Standard in 2005. A revision was issued in 2010, named TIA-942-B.

Initially, the TIA 942 built on Uptime Institute's Tier Classification system, providing additional directives for network cabling topology, power, cooling, monitoring, security, building services, civil works, and many more. However, owing to disagreements over how the standards should be laid out (outcome-based or following a strict set of rules), Uptime Institute retrieved the right to publish their standards from TIA.

TIA-942-B revision is very specific and detailed on its tier rating and the attendant requirements for each level of redundancy and availability.

Details of the TIA 942 standard can be seen here:

https://global.ihs.com/doc_detail.cfm?&csf=TIA&document_name=TIA%2D942&item_s_key=00414811

BICSI

As at the time TIA was working on its Data Center Standard, the Building Industry Consulting Service International Inc. (BICSI) was also working on theirs. The BICSI issued its standard, BICSI 002-2010: Data Center Design and Implementation Best Practices, also in 2010.

In many respects, the BICSI 002-2010 is similar to TIA 942. Many of both passages can be mapped to each other. Only in minute details do both documents disagree.

Also, just as the TIA standard has undergone a revision, BICSI has also updated its standard with a new release: ANSI/BICSI 002-2019, Data Center Design and Implementation Best Practices.

The BICSI standard however does not specify a tier rating system. It only details best practices and recommendations as well as references to external organizations' standards, such as those from the American

Society of Heating, Refrigerating, and Air-Conditioning Engineers (ASHRAE).

Details of the NSI/BICSI 002-2019 standard can be found here:

https://www.bicsi.org/standards/available-standards-store/single-purchase/ansi-bicsi-002-2019-data-center-design

ASHRAE

The American Society of Heating, Refrigerating and Air-Conditioning Engineers (ASHRAE) is a global society dedicated to advancing the arts and sciences of heating, ventilation, air conditioning, and refrigeration to serve humanity and promote a sustainable world. Founded in 1894, ASHRAE publishes journals, whitepapers, technical resources, and global standards that advance its objective, which is *"to serve humanity by advancing the arts and sciences of heating, ventilation, air conditioning, refrigeration, and their allied fields"*.

ASHRAE publishes and maintains a standard that establishes the minimum energy efficiency requirements for the design and operation of data centers, the ASHRAE 90.4 standard. The current iteration of the standard is the 2019 update, the ANSI/ASHRAE Standard 90.4-2019, Energy Standard for Data Centers.

Standard 90.4 offers a framework for the energy-efficient design of data centers with special consideration to their unique load requirements compared to other buildings. The standard was developed under the guiding principle that data centers are mission-critical facilities demanding careful attention to the potential impact of its requirements.

Details about the standard and requirements for compliance are available here:

https://www.techstreet.com/ashrae/standards/ashrae-90-4-2019?product_id=2092750

In addition to its data center standard, ASHRAE also has a standing technical committee, the ASHRAE TC10.1, which is concerned with the industrial applications of standard or special equipment to meet specific refrigeration requirements.

ETSI

The European Telecommunications Standards Institute (ETSI) is a European Standards Organization (ESO). Along with the other two ESOs, CENELEC and CEN, they develop Harmonized European Standards that support European regulations and legislation. ETSI standards are recognized as European Standards (EN).

ETSI publishes and maintains, among other standards, the ETSI EN 300 019 standard. This multipart standard details the allowable environmental conditions and environmental tests for telecommunications equipment.

Part 1 of the standard specifies different standardized environmental classes covering climatic and biological conditions, chemically and mechanically active substances, and mechanical conditions during storage, transportation, and in use.

Part 2 specifies the recommended test severities and test methods for the different environmental classes.

Each of the parts has subdivisions applicable to different systems.

More information about the standards can be found here:

ETSI EN 300 019 Part 1-0:
http://www.etsi.org/deliver/etsi_i_ets/300001_300099/3000190100/01_60/ets_3000190100e01p.pdf

ETSI EN 300 019 Part 2-0:
http://www.etsi.org/deliver/etsi_en/300001_300099/3000190200/02.01.02_60/en_3000190200v020102p.pdf

NEBS

The Network Equipment-Building System (NEBS) is a set of safety, spatial and environmental design guidelines applied to telecommunications equipment. The objective

CODES AND STANDARDS

of the standard is to keep network equipment safe and reliable.

The NEBS was originally developed by Bell Labs in the 1970s to standardize equipment that would be installed in a central office. NEBS-certified equipment and environment give network operators the confidence that a piece of hardware performs optimally and is physically protected.

The NEBS defines three levels of reliability, with Level 1 being the least reliable and Level 3 being the most reliable.

Details about the NEBS and requirements for compliance can be found here:

NEBS Full Description:
 https://telecom-info.njdepot.ericsson.net/site-cgi/ido/docs.cgi?ID=188632236D000001

While some of the standards only provide industry recommendations and best practices, some provisions of some of the standards are statutory. European standards are usually followed in Europe while the US-based facilities follow US standards. Other parts of the world follow either European or US standards or both.

The data center designer should be familiar with relevant regulatory and industry standards and guidelines appropriate to his/her region to design a data center that achieves the expected business outcomes.

CHAPTER SEVEN
TEN-STEP FRAMEWORK

In the previous chapters, we outlined and discussed the various aspects to consider when designing the cooling system for the data center. You should now be sufficiently equipped to be a valuable member of a data center cooling design team.

Now, take a moment to structure out your design process if tasked with a data center project, given all the information you now possess.

Or, simply use my Ten-Step Framework.

The Ten-Step framework is a simple, repeatable process consisting of ten steps. Each step accomplishes a task that has been discussed in this book. The input to the process is information about the business' needs, while the output is a design diagram and the Bill of Materials (BOM) which, when deployed, will accomplish the business goal.

The Ten Steps

The ten steps are described below:

Designing Data Centers – Book 2: Cooling

1) Tier

Determine the data center tier level as dictated by the business need. Speak with the relevant stakeholders involved in decision making. Understand why the business needs a data center, the problems it needs to solve, the outcomes it expects to realize, and the budget it is willing to spend. Takedown the expected power heat sources in all critical areas and the downtime that the data center can be tolerate.

Select the tier level to design based on information from these conversations.

2) Space

After determining the tier level, look at the space which is proposed to house the data center. Remember, it is not only racks that will be in the data center. We will need to position power generation and distribution equipment as well.

Work with an architect, draughtsman, or other specialists to highlight any space and environmental constraints. Arrange the racks using the 7-Tile Pitch Rule.

3) Need

With the information from the Tier step above, determine the need (N) of the data center. Work out the required sizes of the capacity components.

4) Heat Removal System

Consider the environment and geography of the data center location. Consider the complexity of the terrain. Consider the expertise you have available for deployment and ongoing support. Consider the ease or otherwise of material procurement.

With these information, determine the best heat removal system (DX, Chillers, air-cooling, water-cooling, etc) to utilize in your application. Take advantage of every opportunity for economization and efficiency.

5) Components

Armed with the capacity requirements, space constraints, and heat removal system to apply, seek out the capacity components you will use. Work with the relationships you already have with vendors, colleagues, manufacturers, etc. Perform copious research on affordable products available.

Select energy-efficient capacity components that will deliver the required capacity after applying environmental constraints. If you need to combine two or more components to get N, determine any required component or any factor that, if not used, might inadvertently diminish the combined capacity.

6) Schematics

Draw out the cooling block diagram. Decide on the path through which heat will leave the critical areas. Include all redundancies demanded by the tier level in capacity components and path elements.

7) Optimize

Take a second look at the drawn schematic. Every component on the diagram is an additional cost, in terms of initial capital outlay, and in terms of continuous operation. We want our design to be efficient, and deliver the outcomes at minimal cost. Can you tweak the design to allow for the removal of any component or element? Ensure that any removal will not defeat the planned tier level.

8) Sizing

Based on the final approved schematics, calculate the required sizes of pipes, pumps, valves, water tanks, any other path element depending on the amount of heat, and heat removal medium (water, air, glycol, etc.) that needs to flow through the path element.

9) Positioning

Determine the best way to position the cooling units that will ensure efficient hot air return and cold air supply. Determine if room, row, or rack cooling will serve your

TEN-STEP FRAMEWORK

purpose. Decide if in-row cooling is needed. If so, place the cooling units in positions that will ensure sufficient air intake into the IT equipment.

Utilize any possible cooling efficiency measures e.g. containment, air-flow management, etc.

10) BOM

List out all the contents of the mechanical schematics. Include the quantities and measured lengths. Submit this and the schematics to the project team.

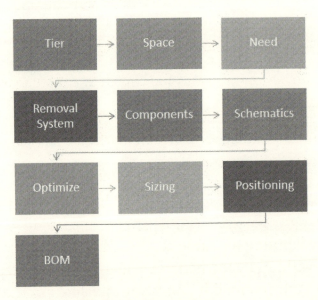

The Ten-Step Framework

Case Study

A company recently invented a revolutionary technology and intend to offer it as a service over the Internet. The company commits to its prospective clients in its service agreements that the service will be available 99.9% of the time. Flouting the service agreements can have legal and financial implications.

For starters, the company wants to set up 60 racks, each containing IT equipment that consume an average of 4kW. If the business goes well, the company will scale up the racks to 100.

The business has identified a location for the data center. The location has a hot and humid climate. In addition, the space allocated to the data center is limited.

Design the cooling system for this data center using the Ten-Step Framework.

You can share your design with me by email at dcbadru@gmail.com. I will be happy to provide feedback. I am also running a course on the Ten-Step Framework where I will hold your hand as you go through step-by-step. Fire me an email if you want to be part of the next cohort.

NEXT STEPS

The foregoing has been a detailed discussion on designing Cooling for the Data Center.

You may find this sufficient for your needs, or you may decide to probe further. You will find that there are other aspects of the Data Center in need of your design prowess.
You may be interested in designing Power, Communications, Safety, Security, Spaces, Monitoring, and Management for the Data Center.

Other books in the Designing Data Center series specifically address the design of all the different aspects of the data center. Some have been published and are available on the Amazon bookstore, while others are awaiting publication.

Join the waiting list, http://eepurl.com/g-ZkNr, to get notified as soon as they are released.

You may need some help on a particular project you are working on, or you might just wish to provide some feedback.

Either way, you can send me an email at dcbadru@gmail.com for your Data Center inquiries.

To your success!

B.A. Ayomaya

BIBLIOGRAPHY

Rasmussen Neil (2017) *Calculating Total Cooling Requirements for Data Centers* (PDF), Schneider Electric, White Paper 25 rev. 3, retrieved April 5, 2018

Geng, Hwaiyu (2015). *Data Center Handbook.* Palo Alto, CA: John Wiley & Sons, Inc.

Mission critical facilities, data centers, technology spaces and electronic equipment. ASHRAE Technical Committee 9.9. Available at http://tc99.ashraetcs.org/. Accessed on May 22, 2018.

Data Center Mechanical. Open Compute Project. Available at http://www.opencompute.org/projects/mechanical/. Accessed on May 22, 2018.

Data center networking equipment—issues and best practices. ASHRAE, Technical Committee 9.9; 2012.

Economizer for Data Centers. ASHRAE. Available at https://www.ashrae.org/resources--publications/periodicals/ashrae-journal/features/economizer-for-data-center. Accessed on May 22, 2018.

Eubank H. et al (2003). *Design recommendations for high performance data centers.* Snowmass: Rocky Mountain Institute

Mechanical: Air Flow Management. Lawrence Berkeley National Laboratory. vailable at

BIBLIOGRAPHY

http://hightech.lbl.gov/dctraining/strategies/mam.html. Accessed on May 22, 2018.

Idelchik IE (2005). *Handbook of Hydraulic Resistance. 3rd ed.* London: Hemisphere

Sharma RK, Bash CE, Patel CD (2002). *Dimensionless parameters for evaluation of thermal design and performance of large-scale data centres.* American Institute of Aeronautics and Astronautics. Jaico Publishing House. AIAA-2002–3091.

Herrlin M. *Airflow and cooling performance of data centers: two performance metrics.* [PDF] ASHRAE Trans 2008. Available at http://wwwhg.ancis.us/images/SL-08-018_

Shrivastava SK, Van Gilder JW (2007). Capture index: an airflow based rack cooling performance metric. ASHRAE Trans 2007

Annual Energy Review 2011. Washington, DC: Bernan Association, U.S. Energy Information Administration

Chennells J (2005). *Trading in carbon emissions—how to ensure compliance.* Energy World

Koomey J (2011). *Growth in Data Center Energy Use 2005–2010.* Oakland: Analytics Press. Available at http://www.analyticspress.com/datacenters.html. Accessed on May 23, 2018.

Data Center Dynamics Data Center Efficiency. Available at http://www.datacenterdynamics.com/focus/themes/energy-efficiency. Accessed on May 23, 2018.

European Union Data Center Code of Conduct. Available at http://iet.jrc.ec.europa.eu/energyefficiency/ict-codes-conduct/data-centres-energy-efficiency. Accessed on May 23, 2018.

Green Grid Library of Resources and Tools. Available at http://www.thegreengrid.org/library-and-tools.aspx. Accessed on May 23, 2018. Offers white papers and other resources on data center energy efficiency topics.

Lawrence Berkeley National Lab (LBNL) High-Performance Buildings for the High-Tech Industry: Data Centers. Available at http://hightech.lbl.gov/datacenters. Accessed on May 23, 2018.

Offers white papers and resources for assessing and improving data center efficiency. Open Compute Project. Available at http://www.opencompute.org/. Accessed on May 23, 2018.

Top 12 ways to decrease the energy consumption of your data center. USEPA Energy Star. Available at http://www.energystar.gov/index.cfm?c=power_mgt.datacenter_efficiency. Accessed on May 23, 2018.

Beaty D, Schmidt R. (2004). *Back to the future: liquid cooling data center considerations.* ASHRAE.

BIBLIOGRAPHY

ASHRAE (2012). *Thermal Guidelines for Data Processing Environments. 3rd ed.* Atlanta: ASHRAE.

ASHRAE (2009). *Considerations in Data Center Energy. 2nd ed.* Atlanta: ASHRAE

Moss D (2012). *Under-floor Pressure Control: A Superior Method of Controlling Data Center Cooling.* ASHRAE Transactions, Vol. 118 Issue 1, p3; Atlanta; ASHRAE

Schmidt R, Iyengar M (2007). *Comparison between underfloor supply and overhead supply ventilation designs for data center high-density clusters.* ASHRAE Transactions, Vol. 113

Sorell V, Escalante S, Yang J (2005). *Comparison of overhead and underfloor air delivery systems in a data center environment using CFD modeling.* ASHRAE Transactions Vol. 111

Herrlin M, Belady C (2006). *Gravity-assisted air mixing in data centers and how it affects the rack cooling effectiveness.* Proceedings of the Tenth Intersociety Conference on Thermal and Thermomechanical Phenomena in Electronics Systems (ITHERM '06); May 30-June 2; San Diego, CA.

Mulay V, Karajgikar S, Iyengar M, Agonafer D, Schmidt R (2007). *Computational study of hybrid cooling solution for thermal management of data centers.* Proceedings of the ASME 2007 InterPACK Conference collocated with the ASME/JSME 2007

Planck, M. (1923/1927). *Treatise on Thermodynamics, third English edition.* Translated by A. Ogg from the seventh German edition. Longmans, Green & Co., London.

Jaynes, E.T. (1965). *Gibbs vs Boltzmann entropies.* American Journal of Physics, 33(5)

Middleton, W.E.K. (1966). *A History of the Thermometer and its Use in Metrology.* Johns Hopkins Press, Baltimore.

Quinn, T.J. (1983). *Temperature.* Academic Press, London, ISBN 0-12-569680-9.

Schooley, J.F. (1986). *Thermometry.* CRC Press, Boca Raton, ISBN 0-8493-5833-7.

Roberts, J.K., Miller, A.R. (1928/1960). *Heat and Thermodynamics, (first edition 1928), fifth edition.* Blackie & Son Limited, Glasgow.

Tschoegl, N.W. (2000). *Fundamentals of Equilibrium and Steady-State Thermodynamics.* Elsevier, Amsterdam, ISBN 0-444-50426-5.

Zemansky, Mark Waldo (1964). *Temperatures Very Low and Very High.* Princeton, NJ: Van Nostrand.

Buck, Arden L. (1981). *New Equations for Computing Vapor Pressure and Enhancement Factor.* Journal of Applied

Meteorology. 20 (12): 1527–1532. doi:10.1175/1520-0450(1981)020<1527:NEFCVP>2.0.CO;2. ISSN 0021-8952.

Fanger, P. O. (1970). *Thermal Comfort: Analysis and Applications in Environmental Engineering*. Danish Technical Press. ISBN 978-87-571-0341-0.

Himmelblau, David M. (1989). *Basic Principles and Calculations In Chemical Engineering*. Prentice Hall. ISBN 0-13-066572-X.

Wolkoff, Peder; Kjaergaard, Søren K. (August 2007). *The dichotomy of relative humidity on indoor air quality*. Environment International. 33 (6): 850–857. doi:10.1016/j.envint.2007.04.004. ISSN 0160-4120. PMID 17499853.

United States Environmental Protection Agency, *IAQ in Large Buildings*. Retrieved Jan. 9, 2015.

Beretta, G.P.; E.P. Gyftopoulos (1990). *What is heat?* (PDF). Education in Thermodynamics and Energy Systems. AES. 20.

Gyftopoulos, E.P., & Beretta, G.P. (1991). *Thermodynamics: foundations and applications*. (Dover Publications)

Hatsopoulos, G.N., & Keenan, J.H. (1981). *Principles of general thermodynamics*. RE Krieger Publishing Company.

Adkins, C.J. (1968/1983). *Equilibrium Thermodynamics, (1st edition 1968), third edition 1983*, Cambridge University Press, Cambridge UK, ISBN 0-521-25445-0.

Baierlein, R. (1999). *Thermal Physics.* Cambridge University Press. ISBN 978-0-521-65838-6.

Clark, J.O.E. (2004). *The Essential Dictionary of Science.* Barnes & Noble Books. ISBN 978-0-7607-4616-5.

Denbigh, K. (1955/1981). *The Principles of Chemical Equilibrium.* Cambridge University Press, Cambridge ISBN 0-521-23682-7.

Greven, A., Keller, G., Warnecke (editors) (2003). *Entropy.* Princeton University Press, Princeton NJ, ISBN 0-691-11338-6.

J.P. Joule (1884), *The Scientific Papers of James Prescott Joule.* The Physical Society of London, p. 274, Lecture on Matter, Living Force, and Heat. 5 and 12 May 1847.

Kittel, C. Kroemer, H. (1980). *Thermal Physics, second edition.* W.H. Freeman, San Francisco, ISBN 0-7167-1088-9.

Lechner, Norbert (2015). *Heating, Cooling, Lighting: Sustainable Design Methods for Architects (4th ed.).* Hoboken, NJ: Wiley. p. 676. ISBN 978-1-118-58242-8.

BIBLIOGRAPHY

Rabl, Ari; Curtiss, Peter (2005). *9.6 Principles of Load Calculations.* In Kreith, Frank; Goswami, D. Yogi (eds.). CRC Handbook of Mechanical Engineering (Second ed.). Boca Raton, FL: CRC Press. ISBN 0-8493-0866-6.

Rathore, M. M.; Kapuno, R. (2011). *Engineering Heat Transfer (2nd ed.).* Sudbury, MA: Jones & Bartlett Learning. ISBN 978-0-7637-7752-4.

Kreider, Jan F.; Curtiss, Peter S.; Rabl, Ari (2010). *Heating and Cooling of Buildings: Design for Efficiency (Revised Second ed.).* Boca Raton, FL: CRC Press. ISBN 978-1-4398-8250-4.

U-value and building physics. greenTEG. Retrieved 2016-03-17.

Insulation. U.S. Department of Energy. USA.gov. October 2010. 14 November 2010. http://www.energysavers.gov/tips/insulation.cfm

Engineers Edge, LLC. *Fluid Volumetric Flow Rate Equation.* Engineers Edge. Retrieved 2016-12-01.

Walker, Jearl; Halliday, David; Resnick, Robert (2014). *Fundamentals of physics (10th ed.).* Hoboken, NJ: Wiley. ISBN 978-1118230732. OCLC 950235056.

Dincer, Ibrahim (2003). *Refrigeration Systems and Applications.* John Wiley and Sons. ISBN 0-471-62351-2.

Whitman, Bill (2008). *Refrigeration and Air conditioning Technology.* Delmar.

Approaches to Data Center Containment. DataCenter Knowledge. Retrieved 2017-12-26.

Silbey, Robert J.; et al. (2004). *Physical chemistry.* Hoboken: Wiley. ISBN 978-0-471-21504-2.